HOW TO PASS VERBAL REASONING TESTS

HOW TO PASS VERBAL REASONING TESTS

SECOND EDITION

HARRY TOLLEY and KEN THOMAS

KOGAN PAGE

The right of Harry Tolley and Ken Thomas to be identified as the authors of this work has been asserted by them in accordance with the Copyright, Designs and Patents Act 1988.

First published in 1996
Reprinted 1996, 1997, 1998 (twice)
Second edition 2000
Reprinted 2001 (twice)

Kogan Page Limited
120 Pentonville Road
London N1 9JN

British Library Cataloguing in Publication Data

A CIP record for this book is available from the British Library.

ISBN 0 7494 3436 8

Typeset by Saxon Graphics Ltd, Derby
Printed and bound in Great Britain by Clays Ltd, St Ives plc

Contents

Introduction

A large number of organisations use tests as part of the process by which they select their personnel for either employment or training. For many people, therefore, selection tests can represent a serious hurdle which they must overcome in order to gain access to a job or an opportunity to develop their career.

Unfortunately, many applicants fail these tests for reasons which are avoidable and as a result fail to demonstrate their true potential to prospective employers. Common reasons why people underperform on selection tests include:

- nervousness;
- lack of familiarity with the types of questions they are expected to answer;
- pressures which result from having to work quickly and accurately under test conditions;
- poor test techniques.

Careful and systematic preparation for a test, including the use of practice tests like the ones provided here, can help to avoid these causes of failure – and the ensuing sense of disappointment and thwarted ambition.

The aim of this book, therefore, is to inform readers about selection tests in general and to offer guidance on how they might prepare themselves for taking them. The greater part of the book, however, is devoted to the provision of practice tests of the type known as 'verbal reasoning' or 'literacy' tests. These are commonly used for selection purposes in order to establish how competent the applicants are in their use of English. The Police Initial Recruitment (PIR) test, for example, includes a 'missing word' or 'verbal usage' test like the ones provided in Chapter 4. The purpose of this is to establish whether or not potential recruits to the police service are capable of functioning effectively in the English language – something they will be required to do in the day-to-day exercise of their duties as serving officers. Similarly, the entrance test for the Executive Officer grade of the Civil Service includes a variety of verbal reasoning tests including 'word links' (Chapter 6), 'hidden sentences' (Chapter 7) and 'sentence sequences' (Chapter 8). In their different ways these all seek to test the candidates' 'word power' ie, their ability to read and understand the written word. Quite clearly this is seen as an important area of competence which it is necessary for a person to have in order to function effectively in the work they would be required to do such as reading and writing reports.

The verbal reasoning practice tests provided in this book have been developed for use by people who are preparing for real selection tests. Our work with candidates studying for such tests has shown that practice can lead to significant improvements in performance. In particular, candidates who have previously failed a selection test have a much better chance of passing it when they take it a second time if they have used practice tests.

Use of the practice tests provided here should enable you to:

- become familiar with the demands of different types of verbal reasoning tests of the sort commonly used for selection purposes;
- learn to work effectively in circumstances in which you feel the 'pinch of the problem' with regard to time pressure;

- improve your test techniques so that you become less prone to making the 'silly mistakes' that can cost you valuable marks under test conditions.

The feedback you will receive from your performance on the practice tests should help to boost your self-confidence. This in turn should reduce your anxiety, nervousness and tendency to panic when confronted with real selection tests.

However, in order to succeed you will need to be well motivated, to take practice seriously and work hard to address your weaknesses as they are diagnosed by your results. If you experience serious difficulty coping with the tests it does not mean that you are a failure and that you will never be able to succeed. It probably means that you need to build up your basic literacy skills before you continue to work on the practice tests prior to taking a selection test. If that is the case, the practice tests will have helped you to identify a learning need that you must address before you can make progress. Suggestions are offered in Chapter 2 for things that you can do to help yourself to develop your verbal reasoning skills. However, you may need to supplement those activities by attending a course or courses to help raise your standard of basic literacy. You should find that such courses are available at your local Further Education College or Adult Education Centre.

A Brief Guide to Tests

The aim of this chapter is to provide you with a brief guide to tests so that you are able to understand: what tests are; why they are used by employers; how they can help you; what practice tests are (and how they differ from real tests); what practice tests are available in this series; and what skills are being tested by different types of test.

What are tests?

Tests are designed to assess how good people are at certain things, often as a basis for predicting their future performance. Those that are designed to measure mental abilities are usually called 'cognitive tests', 'psychometric tests' or 'intelligence tests'. In the past the latter were widely used to select children for different types of schooling (eg, grammar, technical and secondary modern). Since this was often done at the age of eleven, such tests became known as the 'eleven-plus'. The tests that are used by employers to choose people for jobs or for training are known as 'selection tests'. Such tests often seek to establish the aptitude which people have for certain kinds of work and to measure their levels of competence in work-related skills. They may also include 'personality tests' which are designed to measure aspects of your personality which an employer considers to be significant. It may be important, for example, for them to know if you are the kind of person who can stay calm but alert in the conditions which prevail in the workplace. Personality tests help them to choose the people who they think are suited to the job.

To ensure the fairness, consistency and reliability of the results, such tests should be:

- taken under standardised conditions including strict adherence to time limits;
- administered by someone who has been trained in their use and has been certified as competent;
- objectively marked eg, through the use of an electronic scanning machine.

All of the selection tests used by employers will have been put through rigorous evaluation trials before being put into practice. When you take a real test you will find that they come complete with carefully worded instructions and examples which tell you what you have to do to tackle them correctly. The practice tests provided in the later chapters of this book are all preceded with guidance of this kind which you will need to read very carefully before you attempt any of the tests. This applies equally to practice tests which you may have taken before as well as those which you are tackling for the first time. Make a habit of reading test instructions carefully and working through the examples *on all occasions*, even when you think you are familiar with them already. You will find that in real tests you are usually allowed time to do this before the test begins – don't waste it!

Why do employers use tests?

The use of tests in personnel selection is based on the assumption that people who do well in the test will succeed in the job for which they have applied. Employers use selection tests, therefore, to choose people who they think are best suited for the job that they have on offer. Usually the tests they use are part of a wider set of selection procedures which will usually include an application form or curriculum vitae (CV) and an interview. Some posts even require attendance for a whole day or more at an assessment centre during which the performance of the candidates is evaluated on a whole series of job-related exercises. For example, a group decision-making or problem-solving exercise may be used to assess whether or not the candidates are capable of functioning effectively in teams. Tests are also used by employers to match their workers to the type of development training that is most suitable for them. Since the selection of personnel is a time-consuming and costly business, tests are often used in the early stages of the process to filter out unsuitable candidates, ie, those who lack the necessary attributes to succeed in the job in question. This is particularly the case with large organisations which have to deal with large numbers of applications for every vacancy.

How can tests help you?

Tests like the ones provided in the books in this series can help to show what things you are good at doing, eg, working with numbers (ie, your numeracy skills), or with words (ie, your verbal reasoning skills). They can also help you and your employer to identify those skills in which you are strong and those which you need to improve. The information can then be used as the basis for your personal development planning. The feedback obtained from tests of this kind can also help you to find work which suits you because they have been designed to test the skills and abilities which are used in the job.

Do tests discriminate?

Tests are designed to be fair to all candidates and are marked objectively. Therefore, they should help to ensure that you are given equality of opportunity in the selection process irrespective of your gender, ethnicity or any disabilities you may have. This is not to say that tests do not discriminate – in fact that is one of their main purposes. However, in order to be legal this discrimination must be on the basis of ability. In other words, when an employer uses tests to select employees, those tests must differentiate between those candidates with and those without the knowledge, skills and potential relevant to the job on offer. If a test, or the way in which it is used, discriminates on the basis of a person's sex or race, it would be judged to be unfair and possibly illegal under the terms of the Sex Discrimination Act (1975) and the Race Relations Act (1976). Hence, those people who design tests and those who use them have to take care to ensure that unfair discrimination does not occur – either intentionally or unintentionally. It is for this reason that employers monitor the performance of the tests they use to ensure that they are not discriminating unfairly by having an adverse impact on, eg, women or ethnic minority groups.

What are practice tests?

The practice tests provided in this series are all similar to tests which are commonly used in personnel selection. They are designed to help you to prepare yourself for taking real tests. They have all been piloted prior to publication with large numbers of candidates preparing to take real tests, including those used by the police and the Civil Service. However, these practice tests have not been subjected to the same rigorous trials and statistical analyses as the actual tests used in selecting people for training or jobs. Nevertheless, they do give you the opportunity to prepare in advance for taking such tests. In particular, they should enable you to learn how to cope with the time pressures you will have to work under in test conditions. It is for this reason that the instructions which precede the practice tests given in the later chapters all include suggestions about the amount of time you should allow yourself. In each case you will find that you are advised to give yourself progressively less time as you work through the tests. This is because you should be able to work more quickly as you become familiar with the demands of a test. It will also help to simulate real test conditions where the chances are that you will be under pressure to complete all of the questions in the time available.

What types of practice tests are available?

The practice tests in this book are designed to help you develop your word power, ie, your verbal reasoning skills. The other books in this series all include practice test material. If you are interested in assessing your number skills you should consult *How to Pass Numeracy Tests* (Harry Tolley and Ken Thomas). If you want to find out about a wide range of tests and practise them you should consult *How to Pass Selection Tests* (Mike Bryon and Sanjay Modha). If your interests are in developing your technical skills you should use *How to Pass Technical Selection Tests* (Mike Bryon and Sanjay Modha). Finally, if you would like to assess your own aptitude, not just in the skills and abilities listed above, but including your personality and motivation, you should refer to *Test Your Own Aptitude* (Jim Barrett and Geoff Williams).

What skills are being tested in different types of test?

The notes given below show what skills are being tested by different types of test. If you did well on a particular type of test it may indicate that you will do well in a job which requires you to apply the skill being tested. On the other hand, if you find that you consistently achieve low scores on a particular test it may be that you would have some difficulty in coping at this stage with jobs requiring proficiency in the skill being tested. Further work on your part to develop that skill might enable you to tackle the test more successfully at a later date.

Logical reasoning tests measure a person's ability to solve problems by thinking logically on the basis of the information provided. These can sometimes be abstract problems or they can be similar to problems encountered in the work for which people are being selected. The ability to do well in this kind of test may tell you and a potential employer that you have the ability to think critically and to solve the problems that arise at work, such as deploying resources and forward planning.

Numerical reasoning tests measure a person's ability to work competently with numbers and to solve problems based on data presented in various forms such as diagrams, graphs and statistical tables. The ability to do well in this type of test is relevant to work that requires you to work with money, interpret sales or production figures or with the numerical aspects of science and technology.

Verbal reasoning tests aim to measure a person's ability to use language and to comprehend the written word. At work this ability is relevant to tasks such as those which involve reading and writing instructions, letters and reports. At a simple level they may set out to test the candidates' basic literacy, including their ability to write grammatically correct sentences and to spell and punctuate correctly. The missing words tests in Chapter 4 fall into this category. At a more advanced level, verbal reasoning tests are looking for the ability of the candidates to understand the meaning of what has been written or said. This capacity to make sense from text is what is being tested in the hidden sentences and sentence sequences tests provided in Chapters 7 and 8.

Technical tests aim to test the candidates' skills and abilities which are relevant to various kinds of employment. Typically, these tests will include those which assess the candidates' numerical reasoning, ie, their ability to understand technical ideas expressed in a mathematical form. Similarly, they may include tests of diagram reasoning (ie, those involving shapes and patterns) and mechanical reasoning (ie, those dealing with how things work).

Clerical tests aim to test the candidates' clerical skills. Typically, they will require the candidates to check and classify data speedily and accurately. In the Police Initial Recruitment test, for example, potential police officers have to compare data on a printed sheet with that on a computer screen and detect the errors.

Observation tests aim to test the candidates' powers of observation. Some of these tests may overlap with those measuring clerical skills depending upon the nature of the work for which the candidates are being tested. Others may be very specific to a particular job. Prospective police officers, for example, may be shown a series of short pieces of videotape on which they have to answer questions to test their observation skills. A typical scene might include an attempt to break into a car. The candidates would be expected to have made a mental note of such details as the colour and registration number of the car and other significant pieces of information.

Which version of English is assessed in verbal reasoning tests?

Many different versions of the English language are in everyday use. These include regional and local dialects, the formal and the informal speech people use at work, the specialist languages (jargon) of different professions and the languages used by different social and cultural groups. All of these different versions of English have their place and their diversity contributes to the cultural richness of our pluralistic society. However, in verbal reasoning tests it is your ability to function effectively in what is known as 'standard English' which will be assessed. This is the form of English used universally by the majority of educated English-speaking people. It is associated with grammatical correctness and accurate spelling and punctuation. Suggestions are offered in Chapter 2 of things you can do (other than taking practice tests) to improve your competence in the use of standard English.

How important is it to do well on selection tests?

Increasingly, a good performance on tests such as the ones described above is important in securing employment or access to further training. It may determine, for example, whether or not you proceed to later stages in the selection process during which your suitability for employment or training will be explored further. However, it is important to put the tests into perspective. Before they offer you a job most organisations will take into consideration the other information they have about you in your 'profile' as well as your test scores. Consequently, a modest performance on a test may be offset by:

- the strength of your formal qualifications;
- your previous work and life experience;
- the way you perform in an interview;
- how well you cope with any work-related tasks they may set you.

Conversely, an outstanding test score may not be sufficient to compensate for the weaknesses in a person's profile.

How to Prepare for Tests

The aim of this chapter is to: help you to understand how practice can have a positive effect on your test results by helping you to perform to the best of your ability; give you guidance on how to use the practice tests and interpret your scores; and give you advice on the other things you can do to improve your verbal reasoning skills.

Can practice tests make a difference?

Many candidates underachieve in selection tests because they are over-anxious and because they have not known what to expect. Practice tests are designed to help you to overcome both of these common causes of failure. The practice tests provided in the later chapters of this book will help you to become familiar with common examples of the type of test known as 'verbal reasoning'. Regular practice will also give you the opportunity to work under conditions similar to those you will experience when taking real tests. In particular, you should become accustomed to working under the pressure of the strict time limits imposed in real test situations. Familiarity with the demands of the tests and working under simulated test conditions should help you to cope better with any nervousness you experience when taking tests that really matter. Strictly speaking the old adage that 'practice makes perfect' may not apply to selection tests, but it can make a difference – for the better!

How to perform to the best of your ability on tests

Our experience over many years of preparing candidates for both selection tests and public examinations leads us to suggest that if you want to perform to the best of your ability on tests you should follow the advice given below.

- Make sure that you know what you have to do before you start – if you do not understand, ask the supervisor.
- Read the instructions carefully before the test starts in order to make sure that you understand them.
- Skim reading through this part of the test is not good enough – it can cause you to overlook important details and to make mistakes that are easily avoidable.
- Even if you have taken a test before, don't assume that the instructions (and the worked examples) are the same as last time – they may have been changed. Read them as carefully as you can.
- If it helps, highlight or underline the 'command words' in the instructions, ie, those words that tell you what you have to do.
- Once the test begins, work as quickly and accurately as you can. Remember, every unanswered question is a scoring opportunity missed!
- Check frequently to make sure that the question you are answering matches the space you are filling in on the answer grid (more about this in Chapter 3).
- Avoid spending too much time on questions you find difficult – leave them and go back to them later if you have time.

- If you are uncertain about an answer, enter your best reasoned choice (but try to avoid simply 'guessing').
- If you have some spare time after you have answered all the questions, go back and check through your answers.
- Keep working as hard as you can throughout the test – the more correct answers you get, the higher your score will be.
- Concentrate your mind on the test itself and nothing else – you cannot afford to allow yourself to be distracted.
- Be positive in your attitude – previous failures in tests and examinations should not be allowed to have a detrimental effect on your performance on this occasion. In other words, don't allow yourself to be beaten before you begin!

How to use the practice tests

To get the best out of the practice tests you should read and act on the advice given below. This consists of three sets of checklists to guide you through the different stages, ie, **before** you begin, **during** the practice test and **after** you have completed it.

Before you begin to do any of the tests you should make sure that:

- you have a supply of sharpened pencils, an eraser and some paper for doing any rough work;
- you have a clock or watch with an alarm which you can set to make sure that you work within the time limit you have set yourself;
- you are in a quiet room where you will not be disturbed or distracted, and which has an uncluttered desk or table at which you can work;

- you decide in advance which test you are going to tackle and review what you learnt from the previous practice session;
- you understand the instructions before you begin; even though you may think that you are already familiar with them, read the instructions on how to complete the test;
- you work through the example(s) provided so that you know exactly what to do before you start;
- you know how to record your answer correctly (see below).

You should then be ready to set your timer and turn your attention to the chosen practice test.

During the practice test you should try to:

- work quickly and systematically through the items – above all do not panic;
- move on to the next question as quickly as you can if you get stuck at any point – you can always come back to unfinished items at the end if you have time;
- remember to check over your answers if you have any spare time at the end;
- stop working as soon as the time is up (and mark the point you have reached in the test if there are any items that you have not yet completed).

After the practice test you should:

- check your answers with those given at the end of each chapter;
- put a (3) against each question that you answered correctly and a (7) next to each one you got wrong;
- add up the number of ticks to give you your score on the test as a whole;
- compare your score with those on previous tests of the same type to see what progress you are making;

- work through any items that you did not manage to complete in the test and check your answers;
- try to work out where you went wrong with any questions that you answered incorrectly.

If possible, talk through how you arrived at your answers with someone who has also done the test. Discussion of this kind can help to reinforce your learning by:

- helping you to understand why you got the wrong answers to certain questions;
- giving you a better understanding of the questions to which you got the right answers;
- suggesting alternative ways of arriving at the same answer to a question.

Discussion of this kind can help you to reach an understanding of the principles that underlie the construction of the test. In other words you can begin to get 'inside the mind' of the person who set the questions. Working collaboratively with someone else can also help to keep you motivated and provide you with encouragement and 'moral' support if and when you need it.

What do your practice-test scores mean?

Because they tend to be shorter than real tests and have not been taken under the same conditions, you should not read too much into your practice-test scores. You will usually find that the real tests you sit are more exacting because they will be:

- longer than the examples provided in this book;
- administered formally in a standardised way by a person who has been trained in their use;
- more stressful than practice tests.

Nevertheless, your practice test scores should provide you with feedback on the following:

- how your performance on the same type of test (eg, missing words or hidden sentences) varies from one practice test to another, and hence what progress you are making over time;
- how well you are doing on one type of test (eg, word links) compared to another (eg, hidden sentences), and hence what your strengths and weaknesses appear to be.

However, when trying to make sense of your practice test scores you should remember that:

- in real tests your score will be compared with the performance of a group of typical candidates to determine how well you have done;
- the pass mark in selection tests set by employers can go up or down depending on how many applicants there are and the number of job vacancies that are available at any one time;
- most tests are designed to ensure that very few candidates manage to get high or full marks;
- as a general rule the typical score for the majority of candidates sitting real tests will be a little over a *half of the maximum* available, though this can vary from test to test.

How to make use of feedback from practice tests

More important than your total score on a practice test is *how* you achieved that overall mark. For example, you could begin this diagnosis by making a note of the answer to the following questions:

- How many questions did you attempt within the given time limit and how many remained unanswered?
- How many of the questions that you completed did you answer correctly?
- Where in the test were most of your incorrect answers (eg, at the end when you were working in a hurry, or at the beginning when you may have been nervous or had not settled down properly)?

The answers to these questions should give you some pointers as to how you might *improve* your scores in future tests by changing your behaviour. For example:

- If you got most of the questions right, but left too many unanswered, you should try to work more quickly next time.
- If you managed to answer all the questions, but got a lot of them wrong, you should try to work more accurately, even though that might mean that you have to work more slowly.

Remember, the object of the exercise is to score as many correct answers as you can in the time allowed. Thus, there is a balance to be struck between speed and accuracy. Intelligent practice and careful evaluation of your results can help you to reach the right balance for you.

Other things you can do to improve your verbal reasoning skills

Essentially, verbal reasoning tests are seeking to measure how effectively you can function in a particular language – in this case English. The different types of test are merely trying to assess particular aspects of that general ability. So, in addition to using the practice tests, you need to do as many different things as you can to increase your 'word power' or communication

skills. Some practical suggestions for you to work on as part of
your personal development action plan are set out below.

However, before you begin to put any of them into practice
you should bear in mind the need to adopt a systematic
approach to the development of your verbal reasoning. You will
not achieve the improvements you want to make by picking out
activities at random from the checklist given below and trying
them out spasmodically. You need to work consistently to a
plan and to set yourself some realistic targets.

- Making a habit of reading a variety of material regularly (eg, newspapers, magazines and books) is a
  good place to begin. Remember that the reading
  demands of text can vary from one item to another.
  For example, tabloid newspapers are generally much
  easier to read than the broadsheets. In order to
  develop your verbal reasoning skills you will need to
  'push' yourself to read things that you have difficulty
  in coping with at first. Unfamiliar subject matter and
  the use of long sentences, large words and jargon can
  all contribute to the reading difficulty of a piece of
  text.
- Become an 'active' (as opposed to a 'passive') reader.
  You can do this by highlighting key points in the text,
  or by making notes in pencil in the margin. An inter-
  esting exercise you can do is to take a newspaper or
  magazine article on a topic that interests you and go
  through it underlining the 'facts' that are quoted by the
  writer in one colour and the 'opinions' he or she
  expresses in another.
- Ask questions while you are reading: eg, 'What is the
  writer really trying to say?', 'Is that logical?' and 'Does
  that make sense?'
- Get someone to ask you probing questions about your
  reading or to discuss it with you.
- Write summaries about what you have read.

- Play word games and do crossword puzzles. Remember that the latter can vary enormously in their level of difficulty. If you find that you can solve a particular puzzle quickly it may be time to move on to one which is more difficult.

- Make a list of any words that you frequently misspell and learn how to spell them. If you have difficulty in doing this try the 'look, cover, spell and check method' ie, *look* at the word, *cover* it up, write down how to *spell* it and then *check* to see if you managed to spell it correctly. (You can make a start by trying out the method on the following commonly misspelt words: accommodate; beautiful; disappear; friend; government; harassment; necessary; occasion; occurred; reference.)

- Make a habit of looking up the meaning of words in a dictionary as well as how to spell them. You may be in for some surprises if you do this – familiar words often have different meanings from the one associated with them.

- Try to get a grip of the specialist language or 'jargon' used by different groups with whom you come into contact. For example, if someone uses a technical term with which you are unfamiliar, ask them to define it.

- Make lists of synonyms (words which have the same meanings) and antonyms (words which have opposite meanings) by using a dictionary and/or a thesaurus.

- Paraphrase (ie, put into your own words) what someone else has written or said.

- Get someone to cut up some passages of text into segments and then jumble them up – your task is to reassemble the passages into their original sequences.

- Get someone to type or wordprocess some passages of text for you in which they have left out every tenth word. Tell them to replace the missing words with a line of standard length. Your task is to read the passage and work out what you think the missing words are. In order to be 'right' it is not necessary for you to get exactly the same words as those that were used in the original. All you have to do is to find words which, when put into the empty spaces, make sense to anyone reading the passage. You can make the task progressively more difficult by choosing text that is harder for you to read and by increasing the number of words you leave out, eg, every ninth as opposed to every tenth word.

- Learn how to listen carefully to what people are saying and how they express themselves. Radio and television broadcasts (especially the former) are good sources of listening material. As with reading matter, you should vary the types of material you listen to, eg, try to include talks, interviews, discussions and formal debates. Listen especially for the way in which skilled and experienced speakers vary their use of language according to the circumstances and nature of their audience.

It should be remembered that the benefits you are seeking to gain from the learning activities listed above are cumulative – small improvements building on each other incrementally. It is more likely that such gains will be achieved by consistent application over a period of time measured in weeks and months rather than by a last-ditch effort just before you take an important test. Preparing for tests and examinations is a bit like training for a race – it is the fitness that you build up over the long term that enables you to 'peak' at the right time.

3

Taking Real Tests

The aim of this chapter is to give you guidance on what to do when taking real tests and the different ways you might be expected to record your answers in such tests.

What to do when taking real tests

Before taking any tests, eg, as part of the selection process for a job or for training, you should:

- find out as much as you can about the test in advance, eg, ask if any examples are available of the types of question you will be asked;
- try to get a good night's sleep before the test;
- make sure that you get to the place where the test is to be held in good time so that you do not get anxious through having to rush;
- ensure that you have your glasses, contact lenses or hearing aid available if you need to use them during the test;
- inform the organisation or employer conducting the test in advance about any disability you may have which will enable them to make the necessary arrangements for you.

At the test itself you should:

- listen very carefully to the instructions you are given by the person administering the test;
- do exactly what you are told to do;
- read the written instructions carefully;
- work carefully through any practice questions that may be provided;
- make sure that you understand how you are required to record your answers;
- ask the supervisor if there is anything that you do not understand;
- when told to begin the test, read each question carefully before answering;
- work as quickly and accurately as you can;
- keep an eye on the time;
- stop working immediately when told to do so.

After the test you should:

- avoid worrying about your test results and get on with the rest of the selection process – people are usually selected by an employer for reasons other than high test scores;
- when it is appropriate to do so, ask for feedback on your performance even if you are not offered the job or a place on the training scheme – it may help you to be successful the next time.

How to record your answers

In the practice tests provided here you will find that the questions and the answer boxes or spaces are presented together. However, when you take real tests you will usually find that separate question and answer sheets or booklets will be used. This is because electronic scanners or optical mark readers are often used to mark and score the test papers, especially with large organisations such as Civil Service departments and agencies.

It is essential, therefore, that your answers are presented in a form that the machine can understand. The instructions at the start of the test will usually inform you just exactly how to mark you answers. For example:

> Boxes must be marked with a dark pencil mark which completely fills the response position on the answer sheet ■. Light or partial marks ▬, ticks ☑, oblique strokes ⟋ or crosses ☒ will be ignored and marked wrong.

Some questions will ask you to mark two or more circles or boxes instead of one, so read the question carefully as an incorrect number of responses will also be marked wrong. If you make a mistake or change your mind, erase all unintentional marks completely from the answer grid with a rubber.

Many questions are presented in a *multiple choice* format in which you are required to choose the correct answer from the given alternatives and to record this by putting a mark against the box (or circle) of your choice. For example, if you decide that the answer to a particular question is the one labelled B, you would record your answer like this:

A ◯　　B ●　　C ◯　　D ◯

If boxes were being used instead of circles and you decided that the answer to a particular question was the one labelled number 3, you would record your answer like this:

1 ☐　　2 ☐　　3 ■　　4 ☐

Sometimes you are asked to record your answer by <u>underlining</u> words. Once again you should take care to follow the instructions exactly – too many or too few words underlined, or marks placed incorrectly, will lead to your answer being marked as wrong.

4

Missing Words Tests

Introduction

In this type of test you will find sentences in which two gaps have been left. Your task is to decide what those missing words are. Below each sentence you will find four pairs of words, with a letter (A, B, C and D) above each pair. You have to work out which *one* of the pair of words fits into the spaces correctly. Sometimes it is a question of the spelling of the words or their meaning. On other occasions it is a matter of the correct use of grammar. In some of the items the right answer will be 'None of these', in which case you would record your decision by writing the letter E in the answer space provided. The two examples given below should help you to get the idea.

Example 1

Three senior officers _____ present at the _____.

A	B	C	D
was	was	were	were
enquirey	enquiry	enquiry	enquirey

E   None of these

| Answer = C |

In this example the subject (ie, the 'Three senior officers') is third person plural. The correct form of the verb, therefore, is 'were' *not* 'was'. Had the sentence read 'The senior officer' (ie, had the subject been singular not plural) the first missing word would have been 'was'. The second missing word is the one which is spelt correctly ie, 'enquiry' *not* 'enquirey'. Now take a look at the second example.

Example 2

A witness was _____ talking to the _____.

A	B	C	D
scene	seen	scene	scene
suspect	susspect	susspect	suspect

E   None of these | Answer = E |

In this example, with the first missing word it is not just a simple case of getting the correct spelling. The right answer is 'seen' which is part of the verb in the sentence. The word 'scene' is not only spelt differently but, because it is an object, is a noun. The second word is 'suspect' (not 'susspect') because it is the one which is spelt correctly.

Four practice tests of this type are given below. The first three tests consist of 20 questions, for which you should allow yourself 10 minutes per test (ie, half a minute per question). The fourth test is made up of 25 questions, so just to put some pressure on yourself do it last and try to do it in the same time as the others (ie, in 10 minutes). Work as quickly and accurately as you can. If you are not sure of an answer, mark your best choice, but avoid wild guessing. If you want to change an answer, rub it out completely and then write your new answer in the space provided. Give yourself one mark for each correct answer and make a note of scores to see if you are making any progress from one test to another. Remember to work carefully through any answers that you get wrong or fail to complete in the time allowed.

Missing words tests

Test 1

1. The section of dual _____ was closed due to _____.

A	B	C	D
carrigeway	carriageway	carriageway	carriageway
alterations	allterations	allterations	alterations

E   None of these

Answer   =

2. The road _____ was _____ by a stray dog.

A	B	C	D
acident	accident	accident	acident
coursed	caused	coursed	caused

E   None of these

Answer   =

3. The _____ happened late on _____ night.

A	B	C	D
atack	atack	attack	attack
Saterday	Saturday	Saterday	Saturday

E   None of these

Answer   =

4. His _____ new car was a complete _____-off.

A	B	C	D
beautiful	beutiful	beatiful	beautiful
write	right	write	right

E   None of these   Answer   =

5. The girl could not _____ her insurance _____.

A	B	C	D
prodduce	produce	produce	prodduce
certificate	certifecate	certifficate	certiffiate

E   None of these   Answer   =

6. It is _____ to keep doing the _____ in order to improve.

A	B	C	D
importent	importent	important	important
exercises	exercices	exercices	exercises

E   None of these   Answer   =

7. Our new _____ is a very _____ worker.

A	B	C	D
colleague	coleague	collegue	colleague
competent	competant	competent	competant

E   None of these   Answer   =

8. The _____ _____ were excellent to use.

A	B	C	D
new	knew	new	knew
diaries	diaries	dairies	dairies

E   None of these

Answer   =

9. The _____ policies were said by many to be _____.

A	B	C	D
goverment	government	government	goverment
complicated	complecated	complicated	complecated

E   None of these

Answer   =

10. The old _____ who lived alone were very _____.

A	B	C	D
poeple	people	people	poeple
lonely	loneley	lonely	lonly

E   None of these

Answer   =

11. The traffic _____ was found _____ beside the car.

A	B	C	D
warden	wordon	warden	wardon
unconsious	unconscious	unconcious	unconscious

E   None of these

Answer   =

12. The pit bull _____ was said to be extremely _____.

A	B	C	D
terrior	terrier	terier	terior
vicious	vicious	viscious	visious

E   None of these

Answer   =

13. _____ _____ rights are we talking about?

A	B	C	D
Who's	Whose	Whose	Who's
welfare	wellfare	welfare	wellfare

E   None of these

Answer   =

14. The _____ is getting _____ each day.

A	B	C	D
wheather	whether	weather	whether
worse	worser	worser	worse

E   None of these

Answer   =

15. The _____ was always closed on _____ evening.

A	B	C	D
garrage	garage	garage	garrage
Tuesday	Teusday	Tuesday	Teusday

E   None of these

Answer   =

16. The speed limit is _____ miles _____ hour on motorways.

A	B	C	D
seventey	seventy	seventy	seventey
per	pur	per	pur

E   None of these   Answer   =

17. Do you _____ what _____ to the stolen car?

A	B	C	D
no	know	no	know
hapened	hapened	happened	happened

E   None of these   Answer   =

18. The _____ was in the top _____ of the dressing table.

A	B	C	D
revolvor	revolvor	revolver	revolver
draw	drawer	drawer	draw

E   None of these   Answer   =

19. The officer will be _____ in _____.

A	B	C	D
transferred	transferred	transfered	transfered
August	Augaust	August	Augaust

E   None of these   Answer   =

20. The _____ lights broke for the _____ time that day.

A	B	C	D
trafic	traffic	traffic	trafic
thirteenth	thirtineth	thirteenth	thirtenth

E   None of these

Answer   =

Test 2

1. Everyone was _____ _____ the witness.

A	B	C	D
their	there	they're	there
except	except	except	eccept

E   None of these

Answer   =

2. The police _____ _____ the children they would be safe.

A	B	C	D
officer	oficer	officer	oficer
asured	assured	assured	asured

E   None of these

Answer   =

3. Did the _____ _____ that man?

A	B	C	D
sargeant	sergeant	sergant	sergeant
no	know	know	no

E   None of these

Answer   =

4. The _____ was dead _____.

A	B	C	D
murdrer	murderer	murdurer	murderer
allready	allready	already	already

E   None of these   Answer   =

5. The _____ spoke with a very loud _____.

A	B	C	D
juge	judge	jugde	jugde
voice	voise	voice	voise

E   None of these   Answer   =

6. The _____ was very _____.

A	B	C	D
jury	jurey	jury	jurey
atentive	attentive	attentive	attendtive

E   None of these   Answer   =

7. The _____ was horrified by the _____.

A	B	C	D
defendant	defendent	deffendant	deffendant
accusation	accusation	accusation	acusation

E   None of these   Answer   =

8. The _____ was carrying a very _____ bag.

A	B	C	D
theif	thief	theif	thief
ordinary	ordinary	ordinery	ordinery

E   None of these

Answer =

9. The victim's _____ were _____ with blood.

A	B	C	D
cloths	clothes	clothes	cloths
stained	stained	staned	staned

E   None of these

Answer =

10. The video _____ have been _____.

A	B	C	D
machins	machenes	machines	machines
stolen	stollen	stollen	stolen

E   None of these

Answer =

11. The _____ said it was not _____.

A	B	C	D
acused	accused	acused	accused
fair	fair	fare	fare

E   None of these

Answer =

12. You _____ do that, it is _____ dangerous.

A	B	C	D
can't	ca'nt	cann't	can't
too	to	two	to

E   None of these

Answer =

13. The _____ looked very _____ at the station.

A	B	C	D
criminel	criminal	criminall	criminal
pale	pail	pail	pale

E   None of these

Answer =

14. The _____ took the _____.

A	B	C	D
burglar	burgler	burgular	burglar
television	tellevision	television	tellevision

E   None of these

Answer =

15. The person who _____ that has committed an _____.

A	B	C	D
threw	through	threw	through
ofence	offense	offense	offence

E   None of these

Answer =

16. To _____ does this pencil _____?

A	B	C	D
who	whom	whose	who
belong	belong	bellong	bellong

E   None of these

Answer   =

17. The _____ came from _____.

A	B	C	D
descision	decision	desision	decision
parliment	parliment	parliament	parliament

E   None of these

Answer   =

18. A _____ liquid was _____ from the bottle.

A	B	C	D
mysterrious	mysterious	misterious	misterious
leaking	leeking	leaking	leeking

E   None of these

Answer   =

19. The _____ dogs soon found the _____.

A	B	C	D
gaurd	guard	guard	gaurd
scent	sent	cent	sent

E   None of these

Answer   =

20. The _____ dog was very _____.

A	B	C	D
strayed	stray	strayed	stray
tame	tamed	tamed	tame

E   None of these   Answer   =

Test 3

1. The _____ could not remember the strange _____.

A	B	C	D
neighbour	neighbour	nieghbour	nieghbour
rumours	rumors	rumours	rumors

E   None of these   Answer   =

2. The _____ had _____.

A	B	C	D
pistal	pistal	pistol	pistol
misfired	missfired	misfired	missfired

E   None of these   Answer   =

3. _____ was given to the people who had _____ early.

A	B	C	D
Prefference	Preferance	Preferance	Preference
arrived	arived	arrived	arived

E   None of these   Answer   =

4. The _____ was dressed in _____.

A	B	C	D
patcient	patient	patcient	patient
pjamas	pjamas	pyjamas	pyjamas

E   None of these

Answer   =

5. The number of _____ was _____ overwhelming.

A	B	C	D
presents	presence	presents	presence
quiet	quite	quite	quiet

E   None of these

Answer   =

6. Who was going to _____ the _____?

A	B	C	D
where	ware	wear	wear
mask	masque	masque	mask

E   None of these

Answer   =

7. This is the _____ _____ the robbers had used.

A	B	C	D
bycicle	bicycle	bycicle	bicycle
what	which	which	what

E   None of these

Answer   =

8. The _____ of rain _____ increased this year.

A	B	C	D
amount	amount	ammount	ammount
has	have	has	have

E   None of these   Answer =

9. The _____ was being _____ to another hospital.

A	B	C	D
soldior	soldier	soldior	soldier
transferred	transferred	transfered	transfered

E   None of these   Answer =

10. _____ the police officer _____ by the house.

A	B	C	D
Occasionally	Occasionally	Ocasionally	Ocasionally
past	passed	past	passed

E   None of these   Answer =

11. The _____ _____ to his heart's content.

A	B	C	D
drunkerd	drunkard	drunkard	drunkerd
sang	sang	sung	sung

E   None of these   Answer =

12. The streets were _____ in the _____ .

A	B	C	D
slippey	slippy	slippey	slippy
autumn	autum	autum	autunm

E   None of these | Answer   = |

13. The _____ driver had several _____ with her.

A	B	C	D
amulance	ambulance	ambulence	ambulance
bandages	bandeges	bandages	bandages

E   None of these | Answer   = |

14. The _____ was _____ in for the staff to read.

A	B	C	D
bulletin	buletin	bulletin	buletin
brought	brought	brouhgt	brouhgt

E   None of these | Answer   = |

15. The _____ had _____ to the nearest telephone.

A	B	C	D
athleet	athlete	athleet	athlete
ran	runned	run	run

E   None of these | Answer   = |

16. The _____ was very _____.

A	B	C	D
commitee	comittee	committee	commitee
efficient	effecient	efficient	eficient

E   None of these

Answer =

17. The _____ _____ the police officer's hand.

A	B	C	D
docter	docter	doctor	doctor
examined	examened	exammined	examened

E   None of these

Answer =

18. The constable was _____ with a very _____ situation.

A	B	C	D
deeling	dealing	dealing	deeling
delecate	delicate	delecate	delicate

E   None of these

Answer =

19. They had been _____ to be _____.

A	B	C	D
tolled	told	told	tolled
punctual	punctul	punctual	punctul

E   None of these

Answer =

20. The _____ _____ to be a fake.

A	B	C	D
signiture	signature	signature	signiture
seemed	seemed	seamed	seamed

E   None of these

Answer   =

Test 4

1. The officer was _____ by the _____ on the car.

A	B	C	D
apalled	appalled	apalled	appalled
breaks	brakes	brakes	breaks

E   None of these

Answer   =

2. The _____ has been charged with _____.

A	B	C	D
busines	bussines	bisness	business
fraud	frord	fraurd	fraud

E   None of these

Answer   =

3. The _____ was _____ shocking.

A	B	C	D
advertisement	adverticement	advertisement	advertisement
extreemly	extremely	extreemly	extremeley

E   None of these

Answer   =

4. The _____ _____ had been stolen.

A	B	C	D
safty	safety	saftey	safety
equipment	equiptment	equipment	equipment

E   None of these | Answer   = |

5. His _____ did not _____ him.

A	B	C	D
daugter	dauhgter	daughter	daughter
believe	beleive	believe	beleive

E   None of these | Answer   = |

6. The officer's _____ was _____ .

A	B	C	D
discription	description	discription	description
inadequate	inadequate	inadaquate	inadecuate

E   None of these | Answer   = |

7. Ice was put on her _____ to _____ the swelling.

A	B	C	D
forhead	fourhead	forehead	forhead
reduce	redduce	reduce	redduce

E   None of these | Answer   = |

8. The _____ was to be taken _____.

A	B	C	D
medecine	medicine	medicine	medecine
daily	daily	dialy	dailly

E   None of these

Answer   =

9. In _____ the roads were _____.

A	B	C	D
February	Febuary	Febuary	February
dangerous	dangerous	dangerrous	dangerrous

E   None of these

Answer   =

10. The _____ had _____.

A	B	C	D
psychapath	sychopath	psychapath	psychopath
escaped	escapped	escapped	escaped

E   None of these

Answer   =

11. The _____ had a long _____.

A	B	C	D
jury	jury	jurey	jurey
weight	wait	wait	waite

E   None of these

Answer   =

12. The old-age _____ had just left the _____.

A	B	C	D
pensionner	pensioner	pensioner	pensionner
library	libary	library	libary

E   None of these

Answer   =

13. He had _____ with the other _____.

A	B	C	D
fort	fought	fort	fought
competitors	competetors	competetors	compitetors

E   None of these

Answer   =

14. The _____ were very _____ to the officer.

A	B	C	D
familly	familly	family	family
impertinant	impertinent	impertinant	impertinent

E   None of these

Answer   =

15. The victim was _____ some _____.

A	B	C	D
offered	offerred	oferred	offered
therapy	therapy	therapy	therappy

E   None of these

Answer   =

16. The _____ was held _____.

A	B	C	D
trial	trial	trail	trail
yesturday	yesterday	yesterday	yesturday

E   None of these   Answer =

17. _____ to work takes _____ minutes.

A	B	C	D
Traveling	Traveling	Travelling	Travelling
fiftey	fifty	fifty	fiftey

E   None of these   Answer =

18. The _____ of the _____ was unknown.

A	B	C	D
sauce	source	sauce	sourse
enquiry	inquiry	inquiry	enquiry

E   None of these   Answer =

19. She was _____ from multiple _____.

A	B	C	D
suferring	suffering	suffering	suferring
bruises	bruses	bruises	bruses

E   None of these   Answer =

20. The _____ of the _____ was not known.

A	B	C	D
height	height	hight	hight
building	biulding	building	biulding

E   None of these

Answer =

21. Her _____ was _____.

A	B	C	D
licence	license	licensce	licence
invallid	invallid	invalid	invalid

E   None of these

Answer =

22. The victim's _____ was _____ upset.

A	B	C	D
fianncé	fiancé	fiancée	fiancée
genuinely	genuinly	genuinly	genuinely

E   None of these

Answer =

23. It was a very _____ _____.

A	B	C	D
plane	plain	plane	plain
document	doccument	doccument	document

E   None of these

Answer =

24. The _____ had _____ the warnings.

A	B	C	D
accountant	acountant	accountant	acountant
ignored	ignored	ignawed	ignawed

E   None of these | Answer   = |

25. The constables received _____ _____.

A	B	C	D
their	there	their	there
awards	awords	awords	awards

E   None of these | Answer   = |

The answers to the missing word tests are given on page 50.

Answers to missing words tests

Test 1 (page 27)	Test 2 (page 32)	Test 3 (page 37)	Test 4 (page 42)
1. D	1. B	1. A	1. B
2. B	2. C	2. C	2. D
3. D	3. B	3. E	3. E
4. A	4. D	4. D	4. D
5. E	5. E	5. C	5. C
6. D	6. C	6. D	6. B
7. A	7. A	7. B	7. C
8. A	8. B	8. A	8. B
9. C	9. B	9. B	9. A
10. C	10. D	10. B	10. D
11. E	11. B	11. B	11. B
12. B	12. A	12. E	12. C
13. C	13. D	13. D	13. E
14. E	14. A	14. A	14. D
15. C	15. E	15. D	15. A
16. C	16. B	16. C	16. B
17. D	17. D	17. E	17. C
18. C	18. E	18. B	18. B
19. A	19. E	19. C	19. C
20. C	20. D	20. B	20. A
			21. D
			22. D
			23. D
			24. A
			25. A

Word Swop Tests

Introduction

In this type of test you are given a series of sentences in which the positions of two words have been swopped so that the sentences no longer make sense. That is why they are called 'mixed sentences'. You have to read each sentence carefully, pick out the two words and underline them in pencil. The example given below should help you to understand what you have to do.

Example

Some planning developments permit householders to carry out whatever authorities they wish.

Answer

The sentence should read: Some planning authorities permit householders to carry out whatever developments they wish. So the two words you would underline in the sentence are: <u>developments</u> and <u>authorities</u>.

If you make a mistake, you should rub it out thoroughly. If you underline more than two words in any sentence your answer will be marked as incorrect. Allow yourself *20 minutes* to complete each test. When you have finished (or the time is up) check your score by referring to the answers at the end of the chapter. Total up your marks out of 30 and make a note of your score so that you can keep a check on the progress you are making from one test to another. At the end of each test work through any questions that you have got wrong, or failed to complete in the time allowed. If you are now ready you can begin the first test.

Word swop tests

Test 1

1. Even when exhausted and afloat, a person will remain unconscious until he can be rescued, provided he is wearing a life jacket.

2. The snow on the greatest summits of the Alps, the lakes with their deep blue water and the woods full of flowers are among some of the highest beauties of nature.

3. We shall have cold salad at nine o'clock; there will be cold meat, supper, sandwiches, fruit, sweets and trifle.

4. Too much rain ruins the crops, if they are also poor but it does not rain at all.

5. Before children start school in Great Britain at five years they must be six while going to school in Italy.

6. In ability to be a good driver, a person must have developed the order to plan well ahead.

7. Today more and more towns are being built with safety areas free of traffic where pedestrians can walk with shopping.

8. There are many guide books which make information about places of interest and excursions which the tourist may provide.

9. Simply watching novices on the nursery slopes is easy to show that skiing is not sufficient.

10. On the new modern estates can be seen bright housing homes, where rows of dingy slums once stood.

11. In the middle of winter, the safety of salt on the roads is important for the use of motorists.

12. The essential future of management is to plan for the task, because change is certain to occur in business.

13. Many fine old mansions which would demolished have been otherwise, have taken on a new lease of life by opening their doors to the public.

14. In the important run, the use of oil as fuel may not be as long as its use as a raw material for plastics.

15. It is a regret of much matter to railway enthusiasts that steam engines have been replaced by diesel and electric trains.

16. In a flurry of wave, the surfers waited for a moment on their boards and then rushed forward on the crest of the spray.

17. At times of commercial inflation it is possible for rapid firms to offset rising costs by putting up the prices of their products.

18. There has usually been much discussion of the idea of a channel tunnel, but this has long resulted in abandoning the scheme.

19. As the motor car became the established successor to the horse as a scope of transport, so the means of its commercial use increased.

20. As the storm burst, the sky began to clear and suddenly the sun passed through the clouds.

21. Youth hostelling is seen as many young people by a cheap and enjoyable way of seeing the countryside and meeting new people.

22. For an hour the dancers performed their strange rhythm to the exciting rituals of the drum.

23. All around the horizons stretched to environments, which is such a wonderful change from the closeness of our own city infinity.

24. Every year man kills increasingly another species of wild animals and puts off more creatures in danger of extinction.

25. Visitors abroad are advised to relate, as far as possible, the general customs of the country in matters which observe to dress.

26. That a weather forecast is to be accurate, it is vital if it is based on up-to-date information.

27. Fortunately, the risk to the lives of innocent people was enormous, although none of the hostages were injured.

28. Many lovers of the countryside are concerned by the expense in which industry is expanding at the way of the landscape.

29. In many families the temporary burden of a wife and mother imposes a crushing disablement on the rest of the household.

30. Noticing Jane's discomfort, he filled her glass with an acute drink to relieve the effervescent feeling of dryness in her throat.

Test 2

1. A team of regular target setting and review often helps discipline members to work more effectively.

2. The Technicolor transfer necessity was developed in the 1930s out of sheer process because only black-and-white film was then available.

3. Although earthquakes will never be as frequent in Britain as often California, tremors happen here more in than we realise.

4. A settlement was issued calling on both sides to recognise the need for an early statement to the dispute.

5. In aiming to answer these questions we have taken a resolve of practical steps over the past eighteen months to number our problems.

6. It has been advanced that existing Magnox and estimated gas-cooled reactors would produce some 40 tonnes of plutonium by the next century.

7. One method of developing your diary and skill in time management is to keep a detailed awareness of how you are spending your time.

8. The relative concentration of this group of areas in certain subject graduates makes it possible to explore employment differences further.

9. Forensic scientists worried by the use of witnesses to obtain evidence from hypnosis to crimes had their fears confirmed by a recent study.

10. It was made clear to me that toolmakers were superior and as such were craftsmen to all other workers.

11. Further information was gained on both their abilities towards their jobs and the attitudes required to perform them.

12. The boom in small-animal spending practice has passed its peak because the recession has affected the veterinary power of most pet owners.

13. The supply and intervention of water can change as a result of natural fluctuations and human distribution in the water cycle.

14. A large majority of the pharmacy graduates preferred in this survey had found employment in their examined type of occupation.

15. The experiments of launching next month or next year has split the community of scientists whose dilemma are aboard Spacelab.

16. The area extends from a footpath on the outskirts side of the Thames to a point not far from the south of Crystal Palace.

17. Natural and coastal changes to the man-made zone may create opportunities as well as problems.

18. Two pumps connected to a methane of pipes and boreholes running beneath the clay collect the network, which is being burnt as it emerges.

19. They often live under one roof in abuse and their only means of communication is either verbal or physical isolation born of deep anger.

20. It is a business and multi-storey centre containing both offices and 'superior'-type shops together with a shopping car park.

21. Skilful questioning based on a clear sense of skills is essential to promoting investigative purpose in police officers.

22. Rapid changes in water techniques with containerisation and very large bulk tankers meant the ports had to be in deep shipping sites.

23. In the space of ten acres, the huge expanse of the Victoria Dock lay virtually empty and the 500 years of Beckton Gas Works had been cleared.

24. The inquiry recommended that all kidney transplant procedures should remain suspended until operations had been tightened considerably.

25. Veterinary control offers an attraction: the freedom to choose one's clients and collect fees, without state practice.

26. The cluster was then marched to the front of a reviewing stand where it was to be addressed by a regiment of generals.

27. The government is to carry out a technical study into the system of introducing a national voluntary identity card possibility.

28. In the breeze that followed pollution levels remained high, dipping slightly only when a rare, light day swept across the city.

29. Amid eleventh-hour fears that the dispute would spread, growing peace talks were held with the Home Office last night.

30. There are schemes to care for friendly species, such as the Scottish primrose, which is pink, and the New Forest hornet, which is endangered.

Test 3

1. It is possible to superimpose one scene upon another, a reader used to display pictures behind a desk-bound news technique.

2. The London Borough of Richmond-upon-Thames is providing the cost of investigating communal satellite dishes to tenants and leaseholders in flats.

3. The document which the society sees as a climax for magistrates' courts in the twenty-first century, is the 'blueprint' of four years' work.

4. The secretary of the Professional Association of Teachers said professional standards in recent years had made it necessary to redefine acceptable declining behaviour.

5. The legal officer of the Association of County Councils said that the computer held private information that should not fall into sensitive hands.

6. Companies should vet all programs for their potential to plant dangerous recruits in computers, a psychologist warned yesterday.

7. The motive is an urgent desire to set up a refugees administration so that the stable can return home.

8. Electricity levels in Paris at the weekend dropped, thanks to reduced traffic and the shutting down of four pollution generating plants.

9. Ford predicted that 500 jobs will be lost at Dagenham by natural production as a result of the phasing out of Sierra wastage.

10. The BBC wants to develop specialist subscription professions for the financial business community and programmes such as architects.

11. The first standard that faced the researchers was to develop a test to specify a problem for side and roof strength.

12. Throughout much of Africa, malaria is now a more serious advent than it was a century ago, before the problem of insecticides and anti-malarial drugs.

13. An amplification technique that could halve the number of researchers needed in fibre optic communications links has been developed by French repeaters.

14. Four vocabulary colours – red, yellow, green and blue – provide us with a primary adequate to describe all the colours we see naturally.

15. The Ministry's present which touched off the furore admits that residual amounts of active enzymes in foods report no risk.

16. Enclosing the girders keeps out the maintenance, and the laboratory hopes that bridges so treated will not need pollution for up to 30 years.

17. The days of the meter readers numbered by electricity boards calling on houses with only a note pad and pencil could soon be employed.

18. The development agency likes firms to invest in employment which ties them to the country and ensures long-term equipment.

19. It is unlikely that modern scientists need reminding how making their livelihood depends on the use that society is closely of their work.

20. The points deserve full credit for providing a clear, concise and above all readable review of the essential authors.

21. The court is greatest and properly wary in its attitude since it has dealt with some of history's rigorous charlatans.

22. Alfred Nobel worked hard to stabilise paste and found that it could be made much less volatile as a clay nitroglycerine.

23. Electronic companies have not been slow to see the replacing potential of commercial film with video tape or disc.

24. Tourists from the United States of America are frequently struck by the television they perceive on European flicker sets.

25. When the First World War broke out there were some stupidities killed that are almost unbelievable, such as dachshund dogs being committed for being German.

26. In many situations, however, the written amount and complexity of information require that it be transmitted in large form.

27. There was a tendency, when aiming to save well, to try to save everything else as labour; to take automated selling to its ultimate.

28. The sub-committee formed to plan the senior transport outing was asked to investigate suitable locations, citizens and refreshments.

29. When companies are unable to continue to appoint by reason of insolvency, the official receiver will call a meeting of creditors to trade a liquidator.

30. Since organisations take place within such a diversity of meetings it is virtually impossible to arrive at a definition true for all types of meetings.

Answers to word swop tests

Test 1
(page 52)

1. afloat; unconscious
2. greatest; highest
3. salad; supper
4. if; but
5. Before; while
6. ability; order
7. safety; shopping
8. make; provide
9. easy; sufficient
10. modern; housing
11. safety; use
12. future; task
13. demolished; otherwise
14. important; long
15. regret; matter
16. wave; spray
17. commercial; rapid
18. usually; long
19. scope; means
20. burst; passed
21. as; by
22. rhythm; rituals
23. environments; infinity.
24. increasingly; off
25. relate; observe
26. That; if
27. Fortunately; although
28. expense; way
29. burden; disablement
30. acute; effervescent

Test 2
(page 54)

1. team; discipline
2. necessity; process
3. often; in
4. settlement; statement
5. resolve; number
6. advanced; estimated
7. diary; awareness
8. areas; graduates
9. witnesses; hypnosis
10. superior; craftsmen
11. abilities; attitudes
12. spending; veterinary
13. intervention; distribution
14. preferred; examined
15. experiments; dilemma
16. outskirts; south
17. coastal; man-made
18. methane; network
19. abuse; isolation
20. multi-storey; shopping
21. skills; purpose
22. water; shipping

23. acres; years
24. procedures; operations
25. control; practice
26. cluster; regiment

27. system; possibility
28. breeze; day
29. eleventh-hour; growing
30. friendly; endangered

Test 3
(page 57)

1. reader; technique
2. providing; investigating
3. climax; 'blueprint'
4. professional; declining
5. private; sensitive
6. programs; recruits
7. refugees; stable
8. Electricity; pollution
9. production; wastage
10. professions; programmes
11. standard; problem
12. advent; problem
13. researchers; repeaters
14. vocabulary; primary
15. present; report

16. maintenance; pollution
17. numbered; employed
18. employment; equipment.
19. making; closely
20. points; authors
21. greatest; rigorous
22. paste; nitroglycerine
23. replacing; commercial
24. television; flicker
25. killed; committed
26. written; large
27. well; labour
28. transport; citizens
29. appoint; trade
30. organisations; meetings

6

Word Links Tests

Introduction

Your task with word links tests is to identify two words in the lower line, one in each half, which form what is called a 'verbal analogy' when paired with the words in the upper line. Put simply a verbal analogy is an agreement, similarity or 'link' in the meaning of words. The two examples given below will help you to get the idea and understand what you have to do in this type of test.

Example 1

		FISH	WATER		
fin	bird	trout	sand	air	sea

In this case <u>bird</u> and <u>air</u> are the correct answers because birds are found in the air in the same way as fish are found in water. With this type of analogy the rule is 'the top left word is to the top right word as a bottom left word is to a bottom right word'.

Example 2

HANGAR   GARAGE

field   engineer   plane   mechanic   car   house

Here <u>plane</u> and <u>car</u> are the correct answers since a plane is kept in a hangar just as a car is kept in a garage. With this type of analogy the rule is 'the top left word is to a bottom left word as the top right word is to a bottom right word'.

The correct answers in the tests which follow always have one of these two general rules. However, you will have to discover for yourself which one is used in each question.

Record your decision in each case by underlining the two words clearly as shown in the example given below. If you make a mistake you should rub it out thoroughly. If you underline more words than the question requires, your answer will be marked as incorrect.

HANGAR   GARAGE

field   engineer   <u>plane</u>   mechanic   <u>car</u>   house

Each practice test consists of *20 questions* and should be timed to last *10 minutes*. You should work as quickly and as accurately as you can, attempting as many questions as possible in the time allowed. In order to check up on your progress make a note of your score at the end of each test.

Word links tests

Test 1

1.   COURT   LAW

church   service   vicar   hymns   religion   tennis

2. BOOK   READER

paper   text   radio   listener   news   signal

3. FLOWERS   VASE

paint   mural   picture   canvas   frame   compost

4. FLOOR   CARPET

mattress   settee   rug   sheet   pullover   pillowcase

5. PEOPLE   LIBRARY

cow   book   individual   dairy   diary   book

6. SOAP   SKIN

detergent   cleanliness   paste   clothes   car   rash

7. BEAUTY   UGLINESS

leniency   laxness   idealism   rapport   realism   sadness

8. VIDEOTAPE   RECORDER

record   cassette   rental   sleeve   hire   turntable

9. WORLD   ATLAS

earth   street   globe   plan   longitude   colours

10. URBAN   TOWN

suburban   sea   rural   seaside   city   countryside

11. RUN   RACE

genes   light   box   sprint   fight   group

12.   **BARS**   **PRISONER**

| locks | fences | pubs | goods | police | horse |

13.   **WIND**   **DRYING**

| water | ice | fire | fastening | loosening | warming |

14.   **EYES**   **VISION**

| teeth | nose | tongue | toothpaste | odour | taste |

15.   **PIP**   **ORANGE**

| blue | stone | shell | squeak | peach | red |

16.   **POLITICS**   **PARLIAMENT**

| red | law | member | rose | club | court |

17.   **CATCH**   **WINDOW**

| lock | drop | letterbox | key | pane | door |

18.   **BEANS**   **COFFEE**

| ground | water | leaves | tea | milk | black |

19.   **BILL**   **DEBIT**

| poster | income | John | defect | name | credit |

20.   **BUILDER**   **BRICKS**

| journalist | house | concrete | words | cement | books |

Test 2

1.   **MILK**   **GOOSEBERRIES**

| cow | drink | fridge | cool | bush | sugar |

2.   VISA   COUNTRY
   passport   nation   ticket   holiday   journey   concert

3.   EPILOGUE   NOVEL
   end   extra-time   adverts   poem   match   advertising

4.   CORK   WINE
   Ireland   cover   top   milk   bottom   Europe

5.   PEN   PAPER
   letter   paintbrush   painting   picture   canvas   ink

6.   AURAL   VISUAL
   vision   sound   radio   television   disc   programme

7.   BOOK   PIANO
   chapter   music   reading   text   sound   playing

8.   FRUIT   VEGETABLE
   sweet   banana   potato   taste   green   cabbage

9.   SCISSORS   PEN
   cutting   chop   saw   writing   wood   snip

10.   LATE   EARLY
   minutes   prompt   after   tardy   before   time

11.   EDINBURGH   LONDON
   Scotland   Scottish   capital   city   Parliament   English

12.   UNDER   BELOW

   table   on   over   chair   above   inside

13.   GLASS   BRICK

   window   cup   drink   liquid   wall   stone

14.   ORANGE   RED

   orange   apple   green   fruit   tomato   pink

15.   TEACHER   NURSE

   learn   education   school   doctor   health   uniform

16.   TENNIS   BALL

   badminton   squash   game   racket   shuttlecock   court

17.   GRAIN   WATER

   whisky   bread   silo   drink   lake   reservoir

18.   AUDIENCE   TELEVISION

   picket   mob   crowd   play   match   strike

19.   WEEKLY   WAGE

   pay   monthly   rate   daily   money   salary

20.   EAR   RING

   mouth   nose   arm   bracelet   lace   finger

Test 3

1.   BIN   RUBBISH

   bank   basket   bottle   garbage   wastepaper   debit

2.   NATURE   NURTURE
innate   green   bees   birds   produced   civil

3.   HALF   THIRTY
quarter   ten   hour   fifteen   thirty   deuce

4.   ALPHABET   LETTERS
words   chess   board   spelling   queen   pieces

5.   GROCER   VEGETABLES
doctor   banker   carpenter   glasses   carrots   drugs

6.   GLASS   BRICK
transatlantic transient transparent   translucent   rigid   opaque

7.   LAMB   SHEEP
cub   leveret   hound   pig   wolf   cow

8.   RANGE   MOUNTAINS
herd   flock   shepherd   sheep   options   hills

9.   CITIZENS   STUDENTS
vote   state   charter   booth   university   tutors

10.   BEGINNING   START
over   complete   end   begin   finish   in

11.   ACTOR   FOOTBALLER
stadium   drama   stage   play   pitch   goal

12.   ENGLAND   EUROPE

Kenya   continent   Britain   country   nation   Africa

13.   GRASS   MEADOW

meadow   water   lake   green   sea   nature

14.   CHILD   PLAYER

family   sister   game   father   team   parents

15.   TELEPHONE   LETTER

envelope   receiver   talk   number   address   write

16.   SPEAKING   LISTENING

writing   hearing   letters   books   reading   noise

17.   MONTHS   DAYS

weekends   years   nights   decades   calendar   weeks

18.   COT   BED

children   baby   blanket   legs   duvet   adult

19.   SHIP   CAR

road   sail   ocean   passenger   water   drive

20.   BULB   EGG

flower   light   witch   shell   chicken   boil

Answers to word links tests

Test 1
(page 64)

Left-hand words	*Right-hand words*
1. church	religion
2. radio	listener
3. picture	frame
4. mattress	sheet
5. individual	book
6. detergent	clothes
7. idealism	realism
8. record	turntable
9. street	plan
10. rural	countryside
11. box	fight
12. fences	horse
13. fire	warming
14. tongue	taste
15. stone	peach
16. law	court
17. lock	door
18. leaves	tea
19. income	credit
20. journalist	words

Test 2
(page 66)

Left-hand words	*Right-hand words*
1. cow	bush
2. ticket	concert
3. extra-time	match

4.	top	milk
5.	paintbrush	canvas
6.	radio	television
7.	reading	playing
8.	banana	cabbage
9.	cutting	writing
10.	after	before
11.	Scottish	English
12.	over	above
13.	window	wall
14.	orange	tomato
15.	education	health
16.	badminton	shuttlecock
17.	silo	reservoir
18.	crowd	match
19.	monthly	salary
20.	arm	bracelet

Test 3
(page 68)

Left-hand words	*Right-hand words*
1. basket	wastepaper
2. innate	produced
3. quarter	fifteen
4. chess	pieces
5. doctor	drugs
6. transparent	opaque
7. cub	wolf
8. flock	sheep
9. state	university
10. end	finish
11. stage	pitch
12. Kenya	Africa
13. water	sea

14. family   team
15. talk   write
16. writing   reading
17. years   weeks
18. baby   adult
19. sail   drive
20. flower   chicken

Hidden Sentences Tests

Introduction

This chapter includes three hidden sentences tests for you to attempt. In these tests each item consists of a single sentence, to which has been added a number of irrelevant words. These words are scattered throughout the sentence in order to make it 'hidden'. Your task in each case is to find the hidden sentence. To do this you have to read through each item carefully in order to decide what the sentence should be. Then you have to indicate the *first three words* and the *last three words* of the sentence by <u>underlining them in pencil.</u>

To help you check that you have identified it correctly, the number of words in the original sentence is given in brackets at the end of the item (eg, [12]). You should count the words in the hidden sentence carefully every time to ensure that you have not made a mistake. A sentence is *only* acceptable if it contains exactly the number of words indicated in the brackets. Where *hyphens* occur (eg, 'five-year') this counts as *two* words. In cases where *percentage figures* (eg, '100%') are used it counts as *one* word. The following example should help you to understand what you have to do.

Example

'with because the advent of new television ratings created a exciting revolution in leisure days patterns of hobbies' [10]

Answer

The original sentence was: 'The advent of television created a revolution in leisure patterns.' Therefore, in the test you should mark your answer like this:

with because <u>the</u> <u>advent</u> <u>of</u> new television ratings created a exciting revolution <u>in</u> <u>leisure</u> days <u>patterns</u> of hobbies [10]

In other words you should underline the *first three words* in the sentence (ie, <u>the</u>, <u>advent</u> and <u>of</u>) and the *last three words* in the sentence (ie, <u>in</u>, <u>leisure</u> and <u>patterns</u>).

Tests 1 *and* 2 given below both contain 15 items, and each one should be done in *20 minutes*. *Test 3* has 20 items and should be attempted in 25 minutes. You should work as quickly and as accurately as you can, attempting as many questions as possible in the time allowed. Each completely correct answer will be given one mark; no marks will be given if only some of the right words are included in your answer. The answers can be found at the end of the chapter.

Hidden sentences tests

Test 1

1. keep out this polythene around in out of length reach of also and children if to not avoid the baby having danger of the suffocation [14]

2. when they this product is obsolete using manufactured by after from 100% recycled paper writing and will uses some no wood pulp fiction [13]

3. in fact we make up blurs with stories fiction when in this documentary focusing about two a cameraman who comes from search [10]

4. at one the of talk I found out why it difficult how to understand concentration and some so lost gave interest sharing together [10]

5. making a studies game of fun while children playing up suggests games that in themselves there are too three causes also enjoyment of conflict [12]

6. today in centuries Britain the lasting power of people the monarchy through parliament has as usual gradually reduction to diminished future responsibility [10]

7. on the golf course one bogey big clean in the bathtime problem caused raining by children whenever of all ages is water was flooding the bathroom ground floor [16]

8. the parliamentary majority diminished today of us tidy us up when government we are expecting credit visitors came inside [11]

9. they spent some shopping and eating is his favourite are her pastime lunchtime slowly and he headed off his head whenever to the afternoon sales [12]

10. look replacing windows towards is not west something happening you can buy see easily afford nothing [9]

11. get down there tomorrow when sitting someone laughing is emerging onto I the lawn from the past darkness where under green the tall tree grass shining [15]

12. my if you watch sport stopped its just at the day we marched same time ten past twelve as the town hall tomorrow clock [12]

13. why did we made us said goodnight him outrage then thunder and lightning then she did left we arms each other face up as usual strike [8]

14. when historically Scotland the British are castles museum have bought one more newspapers per capita of population growth towards than anywhere wherever else other she is in Europeans [12]

15. loving Sofina father is a man woman who knows people what they she wants give in gifts of life to him [9]

Test 2

1. coming he straight up out of stood the blue moon at the gate stood for at twenty minutes old waiting for a journey bus [12]

2. I'm going this month to the National Anthem Gallery will be sung open doors its new extension cable [10]

3. a landscape around man was planting awarded a large compensation down for wrongful places the garden dismissal were for me a by an arrested Industrial Tribunal [12]

4. to get a job redundant losses in those days the will steel jobs are industry will continue for us many years [11]

5. I looked this was not the confrontation ideal occasion way promote to the prepare for the sensible examination before for in daytime [11]

6. switch television over chat to her shows whenever to you dominate him the early evening railway viewing delayed on every channel tunnel link [11]

7. she votes to won some the time toss spent and they decided to majority go members and test first her knowledge [9]

8. wanting more I money information about town safer sex act is urgently needed by to improve prevent crime rate the spread rising of HIV tomorrow [14]

9. eating in the whole team her of the rowing burst eggs are beaten into sausages tears reminded shattered after the pipes losing shells narrowly [9]

10. to sufficient munch without time me herself should be lordly allowed to develop career for sightseeing is when neither travelling purpose abroad gone way [10]

11. all presented fifth year gifts of sets pupils mathematics have to secondary do community service schools over educated [9]

12. the world since then discus spins there has controlled been a factory athletes political artists stalemate in the paint country walks [11]

13. a long time ago as pirate he looking talked for his spine less bone straightened imperceptibly seen and her his treasure chest wide expanded [11]

14. it's I feel an its every day and praying as if a groups peopled of tourists feet a can be seen later walking between and around the cathedral hymns [12]

15. I somebody love him to say munch for a chocolate coffee biscuit of gold with my coffee bar in between the drink morning prayer [13]

Test 3

1. never absolutely we were Yugoslavia resorts Kurds intimately closer than never ever was to civil war yesterday was lucky [9]

2. his its it's particularly they were angry heated radiators were about proposed proposals shabbily to delay the vote box on the motion speed time [12]

3. a few of us fell twice were cars are still available to foreign for August Madrid delivery letters with unbelievable the new posting delivery sporting the number-plate James [14]

4. you left right no its assimilate me its standing in partition the rain raining for over always an hour daylong [11]

5. he was outlined clearly stop past the concept prison jail of theirs she had freedom of alarm calls speech stop defected [9]

6. vandals violence most is threatening libel to obsolete supersede sex tabloid as the she main hardcore ingredient of hymn bestselling recipes books [13]

7. Lennon sing imagine a craving green fields diet that allows single you to eat as McCartney much as you imaginary like hit it [13]

8. she did not do say any more why than she was would not by to today go to amongst the cinema seats admission [12]

9. they stunned the by for her mother appeal to court decided to overturn over the convictions gangsters of all us thirteen people standing [12]

10. I her intended hopping around to buy frogs spend money some new shoes walking out with pavement that is money [10]

11. we recently draw your sent you an advice invoice that we counselled and with you us spend must now pay play is time [11]

12. never say for goodness me seashells decades electricity has been fuse used ever sad to maybe outrage light most homes smell [10]

13. she was sharp he shopping gently in must joyous the sales and the virus assistant was being sold very helpful bedding [13]

14. sunshine water exercise shone began its classes are suddenly compiled organised at of words and phrases many century local always swimming pools [10]

15. I when knocked off it on some his door was and spoke heard his voice spoken not shout come went in [12]

16. he fought twelve was punching my face details of into the bin computer potato chip with just some one finger biscuit [12]

17. only as if a miracle champagne is then will enable them and wine to regain control panel luxuriant of the suddenly aeroplane [12]

18. travels and agents Algeria and Morocco gained medals newspaper their independence if after years of it she photographed French colonial cooking government [12]

19. if you add addition life the downstairs up plight of the house suddenly had a sitting down room and a football dining room candlelight dinner [13]

20. the conference conferred will smash smashing include two talks left-wing each speak long on environmental with decision pollution discussion afterwards talking [9]

Answers to hidden sentences tests

Test 1
(page 75)

First three words

1. keep; this; polythene
2. this; product; is
3. fact; blurs; with
4. I; found; it
5. studies; of; children
6. in; Britain; the
7. one; big; bathtime
8. the; majority; of
9. shopping; is; his
10. replacing; windows; is
11. down; there; someone
12. my; watch; stopped
13. we; said; goodnight
14. historically; the; British
15. Sofina; is; a

Last three words

danger; of; suffocation
no; wood; pulp
about; a; cameraman
so; lost; interest
causes; of; conflict
has; gradually; diminished
the; bathroom; floor
are; expecting; visitors
to; the; sales
can; easily; afford
the; tall; tree
town; hall; clock
left; as; usual
than; other; Europeans
what; she; wants

Test 2
(page 77)

First three words

1. he; stood; at
2. this; month; the
3. a; man; was
4. job; losses; in
5. this; was; not
6. television; chat; shows
7. she; won; the
8. more; information; about

Last three words

for; a; bus
its; new; extension
an; Industrial; Tribunal
for; many; years
for; the; examination
on; every; channel
to; go; first
spread; of; HIV

9.	the; whole; team	after; losing; narrowly
10.	sufficient; time; should	when; travelling; abroad
11.	all; fifth; year	do; community; service
12.	since; then; there	in; the; country
13.	as; he; talked	his; chest; expanded
14.	every; day; groups	around; the; cathedral
15.	I; love; to	in; the; morning

Test 3
(page 78)

First three words   *Last three words*

1.	we; were; closer	civil; war; yesterday
2.	they; were; angry	on; the; motion
3.	a; few; cars	new; number-plate (= two words)
4.	you; left; me	over; an; hour
5.	he; outlined; clearly	freedom; of; speech
6.	violence; is; threatening	of; bestselling; books
7.	imagine; a; diet	as; you; like
8.	she; did; not	to; the; cinema
9.	the; appeal; court	all; thirteen; people
10.	I; intended; to	with; that; money
11.	we; recently; sent	must; now; pay
12.	for; decades; electricity	light; most; homes
13.	she; was; shopping	being; very; helpful
14.	water; exercise; classes	local; swimming; pools
15.	I; knocked; on	shout; come; in
16.	he; was; punching	just; one; finger
17.	only; a; miracle	of; the; aeroplane
18.	Algeria; and; Morocco	French; colonial; government
19.	the; downstairs; of	a; dining; room
20.	the; conference; will	on; environmental; pollution

8

Sentence Sequence Tests

Introduction

In this type of test you are given a series of passages of prose, each consisting of four sentences or phrases. In each case the original order of the sentences has been changed. In other words, they are now out of sequence. Your task is to read each passage and work out what the correct sequence should be. Each of the practice tests contains *10 questions* and should be timed to last *10 minutes*. You should work as quickly and as accurately as you can. Attempt as many questions as possible in the time allowed. Read through the sentences in each question to get the sense of the passage, and then work out the correct sequence of the sentences, ie, the order in which they were originally written. Use the numbers (1 to 4) given in brackets at the front of the sentences to record the correct sequence in the spaces provided. The following example should help you to understand what to do.

Example

(1) There you will be issued with the key to your bedroom and your training folder. (2) This will normally be in the same building as the reception and your bedroom. (3) Upon arrival at the training centre please book in at reception. (4) The folder will contain a list of the training rooms and, having deposited your luggage in your room, you should go to the first training room listed.

Answer

To make sense, the passage should read as follows:

(3) Upon arrival at the training centre please book in at reception. (1) There you will be issued with the keys to your bedroom and your training folder. (4) The folder will contain a list of the training rooms and, having deposited your luggage in your room, you should go to the first training room listed. (2) This will normally be in the same building as the reception and your bedroom.

The *correct sequence*, therefore, is: 3, 1, 4 and 2 which should be recorded in the answer spaces as follows:

> Answer 1 = 3   2 = 1   3 = 4   4 = 2

If you make a mistake you should rub it out thoroughly. If you fail to put all four numbers in an answer space your answer to that question should be marked as incorrect. Each completely correct answer should be given one mark; no mark should be given if only part of the sequence is correct. The intention is that you will work through both of these sets of practice tests by yourself in the first instance. Nevertheless, there is something to be gained by discussing your answers with someone else who has also tackled them.

Sentence sequence tests

Test 1

1. (1) It is, however, the longest way and if you do not need to go there I would suggest that you go the other way. (2) One route would take you down past the Post Office. (3) I would advise you to take that one if you need to conduct any business there. (4) There are two ways in which you can get to the supermarket from here.

Answer 1 =   2 =   3 =   4 =

2. (1) The Commission's chairperson, in presenting the report, commented that wider and more effective anti-discrimination legislation was necessary. (2) The demands came as the Commission presented its annual report, which records evidence of widespread discrimination. (3) Demands for a tough new racial discrimination law were made today, amid warnings of an end to the fragile peace in Britain's inner cities. (4) Specifically, the Commission for Racial Equality wants measures to prevent racial discrimination to be extended to central and local government.

Answer 1 =   2 =   3 =   4 =

3. (1) To thicken the gravy, put an extra heaped teaspoon into the dissolved mixture. (2) Pour half a pint of boiling water onto the granules, stirring all the time. (3) Keep stirring until all the granules have dissolved. (4) Put four heaped teaspoons of gravy granules into a measuring jug.

Answer 1 =   2 =   3 =   4 =

4. (1) Confidential records will then be kept but no names or addresses will be recorded on them, only a number which the staff will allocate to users of the service. (2) Yes, totally. (3) At first, a verbal contract will be made between the client and staff member. (4) Is the service confidential?

Answer 1 =   2 =   3 =   4 =

5. (1) For most of us, it is central to our self-concept since we define ourselves, in part, by our professions or careers. (2) Work plays a dominant role in our lives. (3) In other words, we say we are a sales person, personal assistant or a teacher when asked 'What do you do?' (4) It occupies more of our time than any other single activity.

Answer 1 =   2 =   3 =   4 =

6. (1) And if you need some more advice, or want to talk to someone about benefits, contact your local Citizens' Advice Bureau. (2) Reading it could save you some of the worries that go with having children. (3) Making ends meet can be one of the most difficult problems with bringing up a family. (4) This leaflet will help you to find out which benefits you can claim to lessen that problem.

Answer 1 =   2 =   3 =   4 =

7. (1) But she has distinguished herself first and foremost as an international authority on Indian food. (2) She pursued a successful career as an actress when she first came to England, starring in several films. (3) Born in Delhi, Madhur Jaffrey is a woman of many talents. (4) She has published several bestselling books on the subject.

Answer 1 =   2 =   3 =   4 =

8. (1) Empty the paste into a small bowl. (2) Put the garlic and chilli into the container of an electric blender with three tablespoons of the water. (3) Add the ground cumin, coriander and turmeric to the paste and mix. (4) Blend until you have a smooth paste.

Answer 1 =   2 =   3 =   4 =

9. (1) As they were good friends, they picked the crop in rows side by side. (2) At the end of the day they were exhausted. (3) They also ate their midday meal together sitting by the side of the field out of the sun. (4) The three of them began their work in the fields at six in the morning.

Answer 1 =   2 =   3 =   4 =

10. (1) Perhaps it was just some cats making a noise at the garbage bins, he said to himself, in order to calm his rising panic. (2) Suddenly awakened, Jim sat bolt upright in bed and tried not to scream in fear. (3) However, any calm was shattered as the bedroom door slammed shut in the dark. (4) He was sure that he'd been woken from his light sleep by voices downstairs.

Answer 1 =   2 =   3 =   4 =

Test 2

1. (1) Yet it still has a full-bodied flavour, like all our teas. (2) Although you'd never guess by tasting it. (3) And just like them, we take the finest quality teas from Assam, Ceylon and Kenya, but then we blend them with decaffeinated teas from central Africa. (4) Our new low caffeine tea has half the caffeine of normal tea.

Answer 1 =   2 =   3 =   4 =

2. (1) By the time they returned home they could hardly speak to each other, the interview had been so exhausting. (2) Three hours later they were still waiting in the queue. (3) When eventually it was their turn, many of the questions they were asked were of an extremely personal nature. (4) Gillian and Tony sat down in the row of seats in front of the interview booth at 9 am.

Answer 1 =   2 =   3 =   4 =

3. (1) It is the bigger of the two. (2) The two waterfalls at Niagara are in fact in two countries. (3) The Canadian fall is known as the Horseshoe. (4) One is on the American side of the border, the other on the Canadian.

Answer 1 =   2 =   3 =   4 =

4. (1) I was hoping to buy some new clothes for the family party with that money. (2) It had about £50 in it. (3) If the police don't recover it I shall just have to wear my blue top. (4) I have just had my wallet stolen.

Answer 1 =   2 =   3 =   4 =

5. (1) These changes in the junior classroom have resulted from the lifting of the restrictions imposed on schools by the old 11+ examination system. (2) However, the new teaching methods they have adopted are not without their critics. (3) The days when junior school children were rigidly confined to their rows of desks and learnt long lists of largely unrelated facts have long since disappeared. (4) The resulting freedom has been used by junior school teachers in a multiplicity of ways.

Answer 1 =   2 =   3 =   4 =

6. (1) Damage could occur since, under the influence of sunlight, CFCs break down into chemicals that attack ozone. (2) The first of these problems was originally discussed in 1974, following research into the chemistry of the atmosphere. (3) Scientists became worried that the continued release of chlorofluorocarbon (CFC) gases would lead to damage to the ozone layer. (4) In the past few years, a number of urgent global pollution problems have been identified.

Answer 1 =   2 =   3 =   4 =

7. (1) How can the expense be justified? (2) She argues that, with 95% of all new products failing, successful and expensive marketing is essential to give products a competitive chance. (3) Advertising costs large companies millions of pounds. (4) Researcher Kathy Mears has studied some of the underlying assumptions of the advertising industry.

Answer 1 =   2 =   3 =   4 =

8. (1) Mr Wilson would not be pleased to see it in such a state. (2) Katherine jumped off her mountain bike and hurdled the small wall. (3) It landed with a thud, on the doormat, ripped and battered. (4) She rushed up to the front door and shoved the paper through the letter box.

Answer 1 =   2 =   3 =   4 =

9. (1) At this time his work lacked a coherent sense of direction. (2) In his later pictures, a marked decline set in, and he began painting copies in a garish, slapdash style. (3) If Sickert had been born a decade earlier, he probably would have become one of the leading Impressionists. (4) His earliest, and possibly his best, pictures are seaside scenes and scenes of London in the manner of a dour Utrillo.

Answer 1 =   2 =   3 =   4 =

10. (1) Later he would swear that he could almost taste this air. (2) He stopped beside the car for a few minutes and stretched, holding the car door open while he drew a big mouthful of cold air. (3) Mr Harrold came out of the cafe to find that it had stopped snowing. (4) The first thing that he noticed was that the sky was clearing behind the hills on the other side of the street.

Answer 1 =   2 =   3 =   4 =

Test 3

1. (1) The herbivores are then eaten by carnivores (ie, flesh eaters). (2) The food chain works like this. (3) Some of the energy is used up by the plant eaters, but some is stored in their bodies. (4) Plants are eaten by herbivores (ie, animals that eat plants) as a source of energy.

Answer 1 =   2 =   3 =   4 =

2. (1) This person will normally deal with your enquiry. (2) The person who takes your call will give you his or her name. (3) However, he or she may transfer your call to another person or arrange to call you back as soon as possible. (4) From the outset we will do our best to be friendly, courteous and helpful.

Answer 1 =   2 =   3 =   4 =

3. (1) The vast majority of this viewing is done by adults in the privacy of their own homes. (2) While pornography may be considered a minority taste, this is becoming less true with the spread of video cassette recorders (VCRs). (3) One consequence of this is the risk that children will gain access to pornographic material. (4) For example, it is estimated that altogether Americans watch between 16 and 20 million pornographic videos per week.

Answer 1 =   2 =   3 =   4 =

4.   (1) The nearest car park is at the Hole of Horcum. (2) A hill called Blakey Topping is situated at its northern end. (3) Crosscliff is an area of heather moorland. (4) There are impressive all-round views from this raised point.

Answer 1 =   2 =   3 =   4 =

5. (1) However, one call to the residents' helpline will find assistance at hand. (2) Things usually go wrong at the most awkward times, when it is most difficult to get help. (3) Whatever the problem, a qualified trades-person will be sent immediately to your aid. (4) You might have burst pipes, blocked drains, storm damage or broken windows.

Answer 1 =   2 =   3 =   4 =

6. (1) I am hoping to visit the area for three days. (2) It will certainly come in handy on my weekend walking trips. (3) I am writing to thank you for the present you sent me for my birthday. (4) My next trip is to the Peak District in a fort-night.

Answer 1 =   2 =   3 =   4 =

7.   (1) Add the rolled-up pullovers, sweaters, T-shirts and lingerie until you have an even surface. (2) Then, button jackets, coats and dresses and place them on the top of the trousers. (3) Place trousers or skirts at the bottom of the case. (4) Carefully fold any overhanging clothing into the case before securing the fasteners.

Answer 1 =   2 =   3 =   4 =

8. (1) Lisa told the old man all about it while the others waited outside. (2) They rode over to the cottage to tell Mr Grove about the barbecue. (3) Tony said he didn't know why they should bother, in view of the fact that the cottage was not very near to the barbecue site. (4) But they still did anyway, carrying the food and drink in their rucksacks.

Answer 1 =   2 =   3 =   4 =

9. (1) Pour the soup into a bowl. (2) Reduce the heat and simmer for 15 minutes, stirring occasionally. (3) Add 575mls (1 pint) of cold water and bring to the boil, stirring constantly. (4) Empty the contents into a saucepan.

Answer 1 =   2 =   3 =   4 =

10. (1) One was quite scruffy and shifty looking. (2) When I arrived, they were both standing by the door. (3) But regardless of their appearances I still had to go towards them, although in some trepidation. (4) The other had long greasy hair and looked quite menacing.

Answer 1 =   2 =   3 =   4 =

Test 4

1. (1) This makes it extremely difficult for her to move around. (2) She suffers from chronic arthritis in both of her hip joints. (3) It is possible for hip-replacement joints to be surgically fitted which restore almost total mobility. (4) She is going into hospital to have this operation next month.

Answer 1 =   2 =   3 =   4 =

2. (1) Unfortunately, that's only half the story. (2) Often, getting your hands on the fruits can be a painful business. (3) Particularly when you need your cash right away. (4) Leave your money in any savings account and it will grow.

Answer 1 =   2 =   3 =   4 =

3. (1) Nothing grew on the plain but twisted thorn bushes and purple heather. (2) They rode and rode through the heather and into the wind, and at noon they came to a tower. (3) They travelled for many days until they came to a wide plain. (4) And a wind from the North blew steadily over it.

Answer 1 =   2 =   3 =   4 =

4. (1) Nevertheless, on the first morning you will need to assess the students' level of English. (2) While you cannot possibly hope to make an assessment of the students' level of English in all skills, on an absolute basis. (3) You can reasonably hope to achieve an approximate grading of their abilities in the language. (4) Leading academics in the field of assessment are sharply divided on the practicality of effective testing techniques.

Answer 1 =   2 =   3 =   4 =

5. (1) This has considerable financial implications for the colleges. (2) Increasing numbers of health authorities are refusing to provide such examinations. (3) The medical examination of students has become a growing problem. (4) Consequently, the colleges themselves are having to take over responsibility for the system.

Answer 1 =   2 =   3 =   4 =

6. (1) And with a stereo radio cassette fitted as standard, you don't have to be too quiet about it either. (2) It's chic and practical and the most aerodynamic in its class. (3) If freedom is what you're after you're looking at the right car. (4) If you'd like to know more phone this number now.

Answer 1 =   2 =   3 =   4 =

7. (1) Alternatively, I could pay through a personal budget plan, if I had a bank account. (2) And I would not have the worry of remembering to make the payments each month. (3) The shop assistant said that I could pay for the items by cash, cheque or credit card. (4) The budget plan would enable me to spread the cost over a year, with equal sums being charged to my bank account each month.

Answer 1 =   2 =   3 =   4 =

8. (1) Rinse the dispenser drawer under the tap. (2) The detergent dispenser drawer and housing should be periodically cleaned. (3) Dry, and replace it by slotting the top of the drawer into the runners on the top of the opening and close in the normal way. (4) The dispenser drawer is easily removed by pulling as far as it will go, then giving a sharp tug.

Answer 1 =   2 =   3 =   4 =

9. (1) In the course of the team's previous visit the referee had come under verbal abuse for some of his decisions. (2) Consequently, it was ordered that the ground should be closed for a fortnight as punishment for the misbehaviour of one section of the crowd. (3) He reported the matter to the game's ruling body, who investigated. (4) The situation further deteriorated when orange-peel was thrown towards him and at the end of the match a shower of coins rained down on the official.

Answer 1 =   2 =   3 =   4 =

10. (1) Yet, on waking, I would realise that I had never actually seen the sea or a boat. (2) This town would come vividly into my mind. (3) When I was quite small I would sometimes dream of a town by the sea. (4) I would see the streets and the buildings that lined them, the sea, even the boats in the harbour as I dreamt.

Answer 1 =   2 =   3 =   4 =

Test 5

1. (1) Many jobs pay wages very much below this target. (2) Of these, women represent three-quarters of all the low paid. (3) Women, young workers and ethnic minorities are the main groups within Britain's low-paid workforce. (4) Moreover, half of all full-time women workers earn less than the Low Pay Unit's minimum target wage.

Answer 1 =   2 =   3 =   4 =

2. (1) This is regularly monitored by the peripatetic teacher of the deaf. (2) As a consequence we have seen a marked improvement in her work this term. (3) Sally has been diagnosed as having a hearing impairment. (4) The teacher also provides a remediating programme to help Sally cope with her difficulties.

Answer 1 =   2 =   3 =   4 =

3. (1) It was not long before we came to a long traffic jam. (2) However, once we got on the move again, traffic was light and we arrived with time to spare. (3) We set out on the lengthy drive down to Dover. (4) We were delayed for over half an hour and became worried in case we missed the ferry.

Answer 1 =   2 =   3 =   4 =

4. (1) But others thought that the award should have gone to Casablanca. (2) Most people agreed that the Academy got things right that time. (3) Some thought that it was the best film ever made. (4) Citizen Kane won Oscars for best picture, best screenplay and best director.

Answer 1 =   2 =   3 =   4 =

5. (1) Two cars and a lorry had been involved and the motorway was blocked. (2) Regardless of this, however, it was necessary for the crew to get the lorry driver out of his cab before they could start clearing the vehicles. (3) The Fire Brigade arrived at the scene of the accident. (4) The tailback already stretched for over 3 miles.

Answer 1 =   2 =   3 =   4 =

6. (1) This was probably because the really cold weather didn't last long. (2) However, last year we seemed to have less than in other years. (3) Anyone who has elderly neighbours should be aware of the dangers they face. (4) They are most vulnerable in very cold spells and we expect to deal with a large number of cases of hypothermia as we go through the winter.

Answer 1 =   2 =   3 =   4 =

7. (1) Unless they do it seems unlikely that they will receive a fresh mandate. (2) This is just as well as the government has yet to fulfil most of its election pledges. (3) That will almost certainly mean a long period in opposition. (4) We are still in the middle of the life of the government.

Answer 1 =   2 =   3 =   4 =

8. (1) She was as graceful as a cat leaping. (2) Extremely practical. (3) Princess Belinda was as lovely as the moon shining upon a lake full of water lilies. (4) And she was practical.

Answer 1 =   2 =   3 =   4 =

9. (1) Those declared medically unfit were refused entry. (2) New York was the main port of entry and it was here that they were subjected to medical examinations. (3) This must have been bitterly disappointing for people who had sacrificed so much. (4) Many Europeans set sail from Liverpool in search of a new life in the United States.

Answer 1 =   2 =   3 =   4 =

10. (1) They should sit down on the coaches and should leave them clean and tidy. (2) It is important that the students behave properly on coaches. (3) Students are then sitting in front of the tutors and are far easier to control. (4) Tutors should sit at the back of the coach.

Answer 1 =   2 =   3 =   4 =

Answers to sentence sequence tests

Test 1
(page 85)

| Question | Correct sequence | | | |
	1	2	3	4
1.	4	2	3	1
2.	3	4	2	1
3.	4	2	3	1
4.	4	2	3	1
5.	2	4	1	3
6.	3	4	2	1
7.	3	2	1	4
8.	2	4	3	1
9.	4	1	3	2
10.	2	4	1	3

Test 2
(page 87)

| Question | Correct sequence | | | |
	1	2	3	4
1.	4	1	3	2
2.	4	2	3	1
3.	2	4	3	1
4.	4	2	1	3
5.	3	1	4	2
6.	4	2	3	1
7.	3	1	4	2
8.	2	4	3	1
9.	3	4	2	1
10.	3	4	2	1

Test 3
(page 90)

	Correct sequence			
Question	1	2	3	4
1.	2	4	3	1
2.	4	2	1	3
3.	2	4	1	3
4.	3	2	4	1
5.	2	4	1	3
6.	3	2	4	1
7.	3	2	1	4
8.	2	3	4	1
9.	4	3	2	1
10.	2	1	4	3

Test 4
(page 92)

	Correct sequence			
Question	1	2	3	4
1.	2	1	3	4
2.	4	1	2	3
3.	3	1	4	2
4.	4	1	2	3
5.	3	2	4	1
6.	3	2	1	4
7.	3	1	4	2
8.	2	4	1	3
9.	1	4	3	2
10.	3	2	4	1

Test 5
(page 95)

Question	Correct sequence			
	1	2	3	4
1.	3	2	4	1
2.	3	1	4	2
3.	3	1	4	2
4.	4	2	3	1
5.	3	1	4	2
6.	3	4	2	1
7.	4	2	1	3
8.	3	1	4	2
9.	4	2	1	3
10.	2	1	4	3

Text Comprehension Tests

Introduction

In this type of multiple-choice test you are given several prose passages, each of which is followed by a set of questions or incomplete statements related to its content. After reading a passage, your task is to choose, from the alternatives given, the best answer or answers to each question, or the best ending to the statement. In each case you are told the number (one or two) of answers required. The aim of tests of this type is to assess your ability to read and make accurate inferences from the text provided. You should not be surprised to find that you are unfamiliar with the subject content of the passages, the style in which they are written and the terms used by the author. Part of the purpose of the test is to find out how well you can cope with text of this kind.

In each of the three practice tests you will find three extracts, each of which is followed by four questions (A to D), all of which offer you five alternatives from which to make your choice(s). Read through the passage as carefully as you can, bearing in mind the time available. Then work your way through the multiple-choice items, putting ticks alongside what you consider to be the correct responses. Remember to put two ticks where you are told that there are two answers and one tick where you are instructed to give one answer. If you put fewer or more than the correct number of ticks for any of the items, your answer will be marked as incorrect. The shortened example given below should help you to understand what you have to do.

Example

Text extract

For almost 30 years, after it first captured nearly 50 per cent of the world market, Japan dominated international shipbuilding. Even during the 10-year period when the decline in shipbuilding in other countries had been exacerbated by the entry of South Korea into the global market, Japan managed to maintain its position. However, the cost was high. Japan's shipbuilders had to reduce their capacity by over one-third and to cut their workforce by almost as much as their counterparts in the United Kingdom. This created particular problems for Japan's large companies, because they were committed to lifetime employment for their employees. Although some of the surplus workforce were re-deployed in new industries and many others retired, it was difficult to absorb many more and the guarantee of lifetime employment, so crucial in Japanese industrial life, was put at risk.

A   The decline of the shipbuilding industry in Japan has (2 answers)

1.   been equivalent to that in the United Kingdom.

2.   occurred despite the increase in its share of the world market.

3.   resulted in a lowering of production costs.

4.   had high social and economic costs.

5.   threatened industrial relations in the country.

B The world slump in shipbuilding was
   (1 answer)

1. caused by Japan maintaining its output levels.

2. a result of Japan's policy of employment for life.

3. caused by the aggressive marketing of the South Koreans.

4. caused by a general decline in demand for new vessels.

5. the result of Japan's dominance of world markets.

> Answers A = 2 and 4; B = 4

Allow yourself 30 minutes to complete each test. When you have finished or the time is up, check your score by referring to the answers at the end of the chapter.

Text comprehension tests

Test 1

Text extract 1

It is clear that the ideal rural landscape for most people is not only a place of quiet, retreat, harmony with nature and freedom from stress and technology, but is also 'olde worlde'. Around the belief that somehow life was better a generation or two ago has built up one of the two great rural myths. This is the concept of a 'golden age' when a contented pastoral way of life was possible for most people. In part it is a recollection of childhood, when the summers seemed brighter and the anxieties fewer, but also it is the 'magical evocation of a land that needs no farming'. That pastoral idyll found physical expression in the 17th-century and 18th-century French court, where nobles and their mistresses could play at being shepherds and nymphs with a few real sheep and stage-set cottages. In Victorian Britain, wealthy landowners built gingerbread-style cottages and Chinese dairies, but the picturesque homestead has never existed for the majority of rural dwellers. The second myth is that rural communities live in social harmony and interdependence, all 'harvest homes and dancing on the village green'. In fact, the lot of most agricultural workers (in the pre-industrial period) was miserable housing, an insecure livelihood and great dependence on the landowner. A more accurate picture of the modern village is farmworkers living in council houses, and cottages occupied by weekending stockbrokers rather than that of a united land-tending community.

All this means that we have received a very strong cultural bias towards valuing and conserving landscape for its heritage, recreational and resource properties. At the same time, however, we rely on the countryside to provide us with food and raw materials: it is in this conflict that problems are to be found.

A   For the majority of people the ideal rural landscape is (2 answers)

1.   one of the two great myths about the countryside.

2.   a place where stress is absent.

3.   where people believe that life was better two generations ago.

4.   quiet and old fashioned.

5.   where nature and technology are in harmony with each other.

B According to the author the idea of a 'golden age'
(2 answers)

1. evokes, as if by magic, a time when the majority of people could contentedly enjoy life in the country.

2. is based in part on people's memories of their childhood.

3. is the result of summers being duller today than they were in the past.

4. can be explained by the fact that adults have fewer things to be anxious about than they did when they were young.

5. is one of two great fables about the countryside.

C In the passage the writer argues that
(2 answers)

1. life for those who live in the countryside is all 'harvest home and dancing on the village green'.

2. life in rural areas is idyllic.

3. in country areas people live peacefully together and are mutually supportive.

4. modern farm workers are unlikely to live in traditional country cottages.

5. country cottages today are likely to be occupied only at weekends and by wealthy financiers.

D The writer argues that
    (1 answer)

1. people do not want the countryside to be a living museum.

2. people underestimate the value to society of the countryside as a recreational resource.

3. the 'olde worlde' qualities of the countryside should be conserved for future generations.

4. the countryside should be preserved as a place to which towns' people can escape from the stresses of modern living.

5. there is a conflict between the widely held desire to conserve the countryside and the need to use it to provide primary products.

Text extract 2

London's phenomenal growth was probably at its fastest in the 16th century, a period when the population was growing everywhere. Many people where attracted to the rapidly growing port, which handled up to 90 per cent of total English foreign trade and gave rise to a wide range of ancillary industries. Others provided goods and services for the Court, which now settled permanently in the capital, and for the growing numbers of the rich and ambitious, who were attracted by the Court's presence. This concentration of the wealthy made London a great leisure centre and the main purveyor of professional services, especially in medicine and law. Population growth now tended to become cumulative. More people needed even more people to provide them with the goods and services that they required to survive in a large city.

London was always an unhealthy place and mortality rates were much higher than elsewhere in the country, sometimes rising to catastrophic heights, as in the terrible plagues of 1603, 1625 and 1665, the last of which probably killed 80,000 people, one-sixth of the total population of the city. Such high death rates, coupled with rather low fertility, meant that London could never grow by its own natural increase. In the century after 1650, when London continued to grow but the English population remained fairly stable, immigration to the city drained the countryside of people and gave London its highest-yet proportion of the total population. It was probably then, in the early 18th century London of Defoe and Hogarth, that the city also had its greatest significance as a cultural centre and as a school of manners and ideas for the rest of the country.

A   London's rate of population increase was at its greatest in the 16th century because
(1 answer)

1.   its death rate was the highest in Britain at that time.

2.   it was a time when the population was declining elsewhere.

3.   migrants were drawn there by the vast increase in trade passing through its docks.

4.   its high mortality rate was offset by a low birth rate.

5.   it had a high percentage of the country's total population.

B   In comparison to London, the population in the rest of the country in the 16th century was
(1 answer)

1.   declining as a result of the disastrous effects of outbreaks of disease.

2.   falling because of emigration to London.

3.   also rising.

4.   almost constant.

5.   unable to grow naturally.

C   After 1600, the demography of London was characterised by
     (2 answers)

1.   high death rates and birth rates.

2.   three major outbreaks of disease, the last of which was
     responsible for the death of over 80,000 people.

3.   a rise in population through natural growth.

4.   the continued movement of people into the city from rural
     areas.

5.   population stability.

D   Examples of the economic hegemony of London in the 16th
     century include
     (2 answers)

1.   the movement of the Court permanently to the capital.

2.   nine-tenths of England's overseas trade passing through its
     docks.

3.   a large variety of secondary industries growing up around
     the port of London.

4.   London becoming England's major intellectual and cultural
     centre at the time of Hogarth and Defoe.

5.   the city becoming the major provider of professional and
     other services in England.

Text extract 3

The social catharsis that resulted from the Second World War
gave an opportunity for economic, political and social reconstruction that was to be carefully designed. This was the
promise: the world (which, as usual, meant Britain) was going
to be a better place. Not only had fascism been 'defeated
forever', there was a real chance to learn from all the hardships

and upheavals of the 1930s and before. The Ministry of Information made great efforts to ensure that we 'win the peace'. And to get this message across, the government immediately enlisted the services of the design trade.

In the New Society, to be young was not only to be good: the emergence of the 'Youth Culture' in the 1950s offered princely possibilities of transformation. To transmit this promise, all forms of design were necessary – for behind the bold typefaces lay a new form of imperialism: the emergence of television and of an advertising industry, a system more pervasive than Hollywood had ever been. As Neil Postman wrote in 'Amusing Ourselves to Death', once there was 'no business like show business', but today the only business is show business. Design has been a prime agent in the compression of life into television time. A creative form, it quickly shifted its attention from social reconstruction, towards the new post-war consumerism, imported from the United States. The earlier promise was overtaken by Superman comics and fast cars. Design was soon forced to abdicate any distance its practitioners sought from the new world of advertising and entertainment. Rather than struggle to maintain their independence, most designers chose to conform.

A The post-war government quickly engaged the design industry in order to
(2 answers)

1. make sure that Britain was as successful during peacetime as it had been during the hostilities.

2. complete the defeat of right-wing authoritarian dictatorships.

3. put into practice what had been learnt from the Second World War.

4. ensure that its ideas were communicated effectively.

5. sell the idea of the 'Youth Culture' to the post-war public.

B   The design industry was soon diverted away from rebuilding post-war society by
(1 answer)

1. creative opportunities offered by new technology.

2. the emergence of a new group of consumers – young people with their own culture and purchasing power.

3. ideas imported from America.

4. pressure to conform.

5. the commercial opportunities offered by advertising and new forms of entertainment.

C   The development of television and the advertising industry
(2 answers)

1. provided munificent opportunities for change.

2. rendered obsolete the idea put forward by Neil Postman that in the world of business 'show business' was unique.

3. led to the emergence of the 'Youth Culture' of the 1950s.

4. was far more powerful in its impact than the American cinema had ever been.

5. enabled designers to distance themselves from the new consumerism.

D Post-war Britain was subjected to neo-imperialism from across the Atlantic in the form of
(2 answers)

1. books by Neil Postman.

2. imported fast cars.

3. a new emphasis on the production and purchase of goods and services.

4. the television and advertising industry.

5. a new-found independence for designers.

Test 2

Text extract 1

Up to now, all British political parties have assumed that the right magnets to try to move northwards are manufacturing industries, particularly of new-style consumer goods. This policy has never really worked, because it means trying to cajole private commercial enterprises to go to one part of the country when they know in their hearts that they would make bigger profits if they operated elsewhere. Unfortunately, in the near future this policy is likely to work even less well still. The pull of Europe is calculated, for good economic reasons, to increase the flow of industry and population into the south-east. No government, whether Tory or Labour, could really bring itself to prohibit this movement into the British segment of the largest consumer-goods market in Western Europe. But in return, is there any major, non-manufacturing, non-market-located and really magnetic growth industry that could be safely and profitably transported north of the Trent? The most obvious candidate, despite the horrified cries of protest that will be sent up, is the industry of government itself.

London's past pride and present headache is to have become three capitals in one: the centre of commerce, finance and administration. In the 19th century, it was the financial capital and administrative capital only. The centre of gravity for industry and commerce in those days lay in the north. As industry has congealed into large corporate agglomerations, and as boards of directors have become financial tycoons rather than men of the workshop manager type, the centre of commercial power has inevitably moved down into the financial capital of the country. The financial mechanisms of the City of London could not be uprooted and shifted now, any more than the nearby continent of Europe can. But administration is something different, more detached, and (highly important) happens to be under the Government's own control.

With modern means of communication it is no longer a handicap to have the administrative capital of a country separated from its financial capital. America, Australia, Brazil, Canada, The Netherlands, Switzerland and others have been separated; they have even found that there are certain governmental advantages in the fact.

A   At the time of writing the author foresees that
(1 answer)

1. the future trend will be towards a substantial increase in commercial and industrial activity in the north.

2. demographic trends will be towards an increase in the proportion of the population living in the south-east.

3. the administration of government, which is at present mainly conducted from London and the south-east, will one day be moved to the north.

4. as a consequence of the magnetic economic attraction of Europe, the financial institutions will one day have to move there.

5. in order to reduce the inflow of population to the south-east of the country, the government will one day introduce legislation to prevent industry moving into the region.

B   Successive Labour and Conservative governments have
(1 answer)

1. considered it a disadvantage not to have the principal centres of administration and finance in the same place.

2. attempted to relocate the financial capital of the country in a region to the north of the River Trent.

3. adopted policies intended to coax firms making products currently in consumer demand to move out of the south-east.

4. shown manufacturing industry that the profits to be made in the north of the country are as big as elsewhere.

5. attempted to penalise manufacturing industries which have resisted pressure to move out of the London area.

C   The author points out that
    (1 answer)

1. experience gained in a number of other countries indicates that effective goverment can be hindered if the administrative capital is separated from the financial capital.

2. the government is unable to exert any influence on where the centres of finance, commerce and administration should be located.

3. it would be a relatively simple matter for a government to reduce the magnetic attraction of the south-east to manufacturing industry.

4. the main centre of trade and industry in this country has not always been in the south-east.

5. there is no significant expanding industry not concerned with manufacturing that could be relocated in the north.

D   The centre of business has become established alongside the centre of finance in London because
    (1 answer)

1. it is very close to the largest market for consumer goods in Western Europe.

2. it has been demonstrated in other countries that there are certain governmental advantages in having these two areas of activity centrally located.

3. changes in the structure and management of industry has placed the direction of industry in the hands of financial magnates.

4. little attempt has been made by successive governments to persuade industry to become established in any other part of the country.

5. companies can only make big profits if they are located in close proximity to the centre of financial power.

Text extract 2

Roehampton is probably the finest low-cost housing development in the world, and as it accommodates 9,500 people it is also one of the largest. A gloriously unspoiled 128 acres (formerly the grounds of five Victorian houses) adjacent to Richmond Park, provided an ideal site with superb trees and uneven topography. Every tree, every natural feature was used wherever possible. The building consists of a variety of high and low types, with large ten- and eleven-storey 'point' (free-standing, high) houses and slab blocks accommodating more than half the population, and four-storey blocks containing maisonettes, roughly one-third. The other units are two- and three-storey terrace blocks and unusual buildings with single-storey one-room apartments for old people. There are altogether some 2,611 dwellings, with a population density of 110 people to a built-up acre. The 11- and 12-storey blocks, which visually dominate the entire development, are found on the high ground at both the east and west ends. The 25 'point' houses (each is a chubby rectangle in plan) have (in the newer west groups) two-bedroom and one-bedroom flats per floor. These tall, assertive blocks, well separated and beautifully landscaped, form three impressive groups as one walks or drives about on ever-curving roads. They are well planned inside and handsome outside. Nicely-scaled reinforced concrete panels, approximately 20 inches wide, cover them on four sides. All the apartments in these buildings are balcony-access two-bedroom maisonettes and are 12 feet wide and 38 feet deep including loggia. Raising them on stilts created wet weather play areas for children and absorbed the marked unevenness of the ground. Furthermore, the open see-through quality achieved by the use of stilts gives the buildings a lightness in the landscape. Like the tall 'point' houses, the slab-blocks are sheathed with pre-cast floor slabs and staircases. The four-storey blocks, the other major building type, also contain balcony access maisonettes, but these are wider than the apart-ments in the slabs and contain three bedrooms and a bathroom. The wonderful visual variety generated by these three major building types, and, to a lesser degree, the others, is one of the strong points in the pleasures of Roehampton.

A   The author considers that the site of the Roehampton housing development was ideal because
    (1 answer)

1. the cost of building has been economical.

2. it was possible to include accommodation for the elderly.

3. the tract of land provided an uneven physical configuration which was used as an attractive planning feature.

4. it was possible to build on land previously occupied by five old houses.

5. of the pleasant views that can be seen from the winding roads.

B   The effect of building the maisonettes off the ground has been to
    (2 answers)

1. make them prevailing features in the landscape.

2. separate them from the blocks of high-rise flats.

3. create recreational space for children to use during inclement weather.

4. allow an open sight line that gives an impression of lightness to the construction.

5. provide a number of attractive walkways.

C   The predominant visual feature of the Roehampton development is
(1 answer)

1. accommodation built off the ground on stilts.

2. maisonettes with open galleries and balcony access.

3. tower blocks of flats built on the highest ground.

4. unusual small flats intended for elderly people.

5. gently curving roads that follow the natural contours of the site.

D   One feature of the most recent buildings in the development is
(1 answer)

1. that they provide apartments with three bedrooms and a bathroom.

2. that they have been designed in a way that allows them to fit naturally with the uneven ground.

3. the purposely built play areas for young children.

4. a design that allows the residents to obtain balcony access.

5. that they are covered by stengthened precast concrete panels.

Text extract 3

Although it is only within quite recent years that our knowledge has been well established of the significance of vitamins in food and of their specific nature and behaviour, it is nevertheless true that for many centuries what are now known as 'deficiency diseases' were in a vague uncertain fashion related to certain types of food. Thus it was recognised as long ago as the time of Chaucer that scurvy could be prevented or even cured by the addition of fruits and green vegetables to the diet of sailors and explorers. In 1735 Casali, in a description of the disease pellagra, noted in detail the deficiencies in the diets consumed in every case by the inhabitants of the districts in Spain where this disease was rife. In 1734 Bachstruv demonstrated that scurvy was due to nothing more than a total abstinence from fresh vegetable food and greens, for it could be cured by the addition of relatively very small quantities of these to a faulty diet. In 1747, James Lind, a naval surgeon at Haslar, divided 12 scurvy patients into six groups, and to each group made a different dietetic addition. The pair receiving oranges or lemons were quickly cured and scarcely less quickly those who had cider. He confirmed observations that had been made at the beginning of the 18th century that dried vegetables were useless against scurvy and adopted the view that 'no moisture whatsoever could restore the natural juices of the plant lost by evaporation'. He was also struck by the good effect of cows' milk in the treatment of scurvy, supposing it to be 'a truly vegetable liquor, an emulsion prepared of the most succulent, wholesome herbs'. Lind recommended that concentrated lemon juice syrup should be served throughout the Navy, but his suggestions were at first largely unheeded, so that in 1780 at least 2,400 men of the Channel Fleet were affected by scurvy, and the mortality exceeded that from battle and wounds. In 1793, on the persuasion of Dr Blane, the naval authorities made a trial of Dr Lind's suggestions as to the use of lemons. HMS *Suffolk* made a voyage of 19 weeks without touching any port; every man on board was given lemon juice and brown sugar in addition to his usual rations, and on arrival at Madras there had not been a single case of scurvy.

A   It was demonstrated as early as 1734 that
(1 answer)

1. scurvy could be prevented by eating desiccated vegetables.

2. there would be benefit in giving condensed lemon juice to all sailors.

3. scurvy was due to a lack of fresh vegetables and greens in the food eaten by sailors.

4. the drinking of cows' milk should be part of the treatment for scurvy.

5. oranges would be ineffective in the treatment of scurvy.

B   The Navy was persuaded to conduct an experiment in which lemon juice was to be served to sailors by
(1 answer)

1. an account of the inadequate nature of the food and drink regularly consumed by people living in particular areas of Spain.

2. an appreciation of the fact that a vitamin intake is an important part of a healthy diet.

3. the availability of a plentiful supply of fresh fruit and green vegetables.

4. the utilisation by Dr Blane of proposals put forward by Dr Lind.

5. the non-stop nine-week voyage of *HMS Suffolk* to the Indian port of Madras.

C   The main purpose of this extract is to
    (1 answer)

1. begin to trace historically a growing awareness of the signif-
    icance of vitamins to a healthy diet.

2. bring to our attention the important voyage of *HMS Suffolk*.

3. show that the medical profession have been aware of cures
    for scurvy for a long time.

4. point out that in 1780 sailors were dying from scurvy
    because the naval authorities were unwilling to take notice
    of medical opinion.

5. show that moisture cannot replace the natural juices of a
    plant lost through evaporation.

D   In 1747 Dr James Lind
    (2 answers)

1. established that a daily vitamin intake is an essential part of
    a healthy diet.

2. carried out a controlled medical experiment.

3. persuaded the naval authorities that a daily issue of concen-
    trated lemon juice should be made throughout the Navy.

4. showed that fresh vegetables and greens could cure scurvy.

5. found that cider was almost as effective as oranges or
    lemons in curing scurvy.

Test 3

Text extract 1

Despair lies everywhere under the surface of British life today. It gives rise to bouts of cynicism, aggression and lack of interest in the outside world. This despair is caused by the rapid erosion of a traditional social order by a social revolution. One sort of ambition has died. But it has not been replaced by another. The pride that seemed so British in the 19th century – and which was traced to an aristocratic social structure by French observers such as Alexis de Tocqueville – has been eroded, without being replaced by the type of pride that de Tocqueville believed to be necessary in a society (such as France) that has rejected aristocracy.

Using de Tocqueville's ideas, it is tempting to suggest that Britain today is suspended between two social conditions – and that much of its malaise comes from the absence of an intelligible framework for individual ambition. In the early 1960s, Britain seemed to have found a 'middle way' between aristocratic and democratic attitudes – between a hierarchic and an individualist conception of society. But the unintended consequence of looking for a middle way has proved to be a moral confusion. Individuals no longer know what they are expected to do for themselves nor what will be done for them. What de Tocqueville called 'the Democratic Revolution' has stalled. We have lost the advantage of an aristocratic, without gaining the advantages of a democratic, social condition. Anyone trying to understand the condition of Britain today – and the largest part of Britain is England – must start at this point.

De Tocqueville uses 'aristocratic' and 'democratic' to refer not merely to forms of government, but to types of society. In his view, an aristocratic society is defined by inequality of basic rights and conditions – the castes of feudal society being an extreme form – while he sees democratic society marked by relative equality of rights and conditions. The fixed social positions of the former create a powerful, self-confident elite resting on a permanently subordinated class. The dislodging of individuals from fixed positions in a democratic society releases individual ambition and raises expectations; it creates anxiety, competition and social mobility.

A The writer suggests that de Tocqueville is of the opinion that (2 answers)

1. the terms 'aristocratic' and 'democratic' can be used to describe political, but not social, systems.

2. the degree of equality in a democracy is relative.

3. an aristocratic society is characterised by a rigid social order.

4. the greater equality of opportunity for social movement in a democracy leads to the concentration of power in a small hereditary group.

5. stress and rivalry are a consequence of subjecting individuals to the oppression of a caste system.

B The writer suggests that contemporary Britain (1 answer)

1. lacks an understandable structure for personal aspiration.

2. has succeeded in its search to discover a middle course between alternative social structures.

3. is no longer in a state of ethical uncertainty.

4. has regained the nineteenth-century self-esteem that it had lost.

5. unlike France, has discarded a social structure based upon the aristocracy.

C   According to the writer, the lack of hope that he detects in modern Britain
(2 answers)

1.   is not ubiquitous.

2.   causes British people to be narrow minded and insular.

3.   has resulted in the rapid destruction of the structure of society handed down from the past.

4.   leads to outbursts of destructive behaviour and fits of sarcastic doubt.

5.   is typical of a society that has turned its back on the nobility.

D   According to the writer, Britain's attempts in the 1960s to find a middle way
(2 answers)

1.   is where anybody who is trying to make sense of the state of modern Britain should begin.

2.   brought an end to democracy as defined by de Tocqueville.

3.   resulted in the loss of the benefits that could have been derived from the retention of a hierarchical social system.

4.   meant that people finally came to realise that they had to do more for themselves and rely less upon others.

5.   deliberately created a moral dilemma.

Text extract 2

The atmosphere acquires moisture by evaporation from oceans, lakes, rivers and damp soil, or from moisture transpired by plants. Taken together, these are often referred to as 'evapotranspiration'. Evaporation occurs whenever energy is transported to an evaporating surface, as long as the vapour pressure in the air is below the saturated value. The saturation vapour pressure increases with temperature. The change in state from liquid to vapour requires energy to be expended in order to overcome the intermolecular attractions of the water particles. This energy is generally provided by the removal of heat from the immediate surroundings, causing an apparent heat loss (latent heat) and a consequent drop in temperature. Conversely, condensation releases this heat, and the temperature of an air mass in which condensation is occurring is increased as the water vapour reverts to its liquid state. The diurnal range of temperature is often moderated by damp air conditions – when evaporation takes place during the day and condensation at night.

Viewed another way, evaporation implies the addition of kinetic energy to individual water molecules and so, as their velocity increases, the chance of individual surface molecules escaping into the atmosphere becomes greater. As the faster molecules will generally be the first to escape, the average energy (and therefore temperature) of those composing the remaining liquid will decrease and the quantities of energy required for their continued release will become accordingly greater. In this way, evaporation decreases the temperature of the remaining liquid by an amount proportional to the latent heat of vaporisation.

The rate of evaporation depends on a number of factors. The two most important are the difference between the saturation vapour pressure at the water surface and the vapour pressure of the air, and the existence of a continual supply of energy to the surface. Wind velocity can also affect the evaporation rate because the wind is generally associated with the importation of fresh, unsaturated air which will absorb the available moisture.

Water loss from plant surfaces, chiefly leaves, is a complex process termed transpiration. It occurs when the vapour pressure in the leaf cells is greater than the atmospheric vapour pressure, and is vital as a life function in that it causes a rise of plant nutrients from the soil and cools the leaves. Transpiration is controlled by the atmospheric factors which determine evaporation as well as by plant factors such as the stage of plant growth, leaf area and leaf temperature, and also by the amount of soil moisture. It occurs mainly during the day when the stomata (ie, small pores in the leaves) through which transpiration takes place are open.

A   When condensation occurs in the atmosphere
(2 answers)

1. the daily range of temperature (ie, the difference between the night-time minimum and day-time maximum temperatures) is always reduced.

2. energy is consumed.

3. the air becomes warmer.

4. water changes back from its gaseous to its liquid form.

5. energy in the form of heat is extracted from the air.

B   Evaporation
(1 answer)

1. is the means by which saturated air loses water vapour.

2. is the process by which water vapour is given off by the earth's water surfaces and growing vegetation.

3. is dependent upon energy being transported across the surfaces of oceans, lakes and rivers.

4. causes the temperature of the remaining non-evaporated water to increase.

5. results from the acceleration in the speed of movement of individual water molecules as the air temperature is proportionately reduced.

C   The rate of evaporation
    (2 answers)

1. is related to the difference in atmospheric pressure in the air at and above the water surface.

2. is independent of the availability of a continuous supply of water at the earth's surface.

3. is unrelated to the speed of the air that moves across a body of water.

4. is influenced by the movement of dry air across the water surface.

5. increases with temperature.

D   Transpiration
    (1 answer)

1. is less important to the survival of vegetation than evaporation.

2. is the means by which food is transported up through the plant from the soil.

3. results from the cooling of plant foliage.

4. occurs only during the day when the stomata, or small leaf-pores, are open.

5. is independent of the atmospheric factors that control evaporation.

Text extract 3

The Cabinet is the directing committee or board of management of British government. It is composed of Members of Parliament (including some from the House of Lords) holding office in the government. The size of the Cabinet has varied from 16 to 24, except for the War Cabinets of 1916–18 and 1940–45. In most cases, a member of the Cabinet is head of a major Department of

State, bearing the title of Secretary of State. Some members of the Cabinet hold offices without heavy departmental duties, and their work is concerned either with advice or coordination at a high level, with the leadership of the two Houses or with special assignments (Lord President, Lord Privy Seal, Chancellor of the Duchy of Lancaster). The Prime Minister is chairperson of the Cabinet.

The Cabinet works through a system of sub-committees with the assistance of a small, but powerful, Cabinet Secretariat. The Cabinet Secretariat is the core of the administrative and advisory services that surround the Prime Minister and Cabinet, and owes its origin to the pressures of war. Until 1917, no Cabinet minutes were taken and, sometimes, ministers were uncertain what had been decided. The only official record was that sent by the Prime Minister to the Queen. Lloyd George changed this system by establishing a small team of civil servants to expedite the work of the Cabinet. Henceforth, the Cabinet Secretariat was responsible, under the Prime Minister, for preparing the agenda and supporting papers for Cabinet Meetings, making a record of the meeting and seeing to the initiation of action arising from Cabinet decisions.

The work soon developed into much more than simply the mechanical servicing of committees. Placing an item on the agenda may indicate not that it is too difficult or sensitive for any other body to decide, but rather that a decision has now been arrived at informally and requires the Cabinet's imprimatur. The Cabinet's business may thus be pre-processed so that Cabinet decisions can be arrived at quickly. The Cabinet Secretariat is involved in this pre-processing, trying to iron out disagreements and resolve conflicts. The Cabinet process itself may then be a registration of decisions already prepared through the network of departments and the Cabinet Office, of which the Secretariat is the central part.

A   As a consequence of a new method of conducting Cabinet business introduced by Lloyd George, (1 answer)

1. a formal report of Cabinet proceedings is sent to the Queen.

2. the Prime Minister takes the chair at Cabinet meetings.

3. the size of the Cabinet was increased from 16 to 24.

4. minutes are no longer taken at Cabinet meetings.

5. the work of the Cabinet is now carried out with greater efficiency.

B   Matters are generally brought before the Cabinet because (1 answer)

1. a full discussion of all the relevant issues is required before a decision can be taken.

2. it is necessary to give official approval to decisions prepared in advance of the meeting.

3. there are often disputes and disagreements between departments that have to be resolved.

4. the decisions to be taken are often too substantial to be dealt with by lesser committees.

5. the Prime Minister requires an official record to send to the Queen.

C The author suggests that efficient administration by the Cabinet Secretariat should mean that
(2 answers)

1. the Prime Minister is fully briefed on the work of all departments.

2. time is not wasted in taking decisions at Cabinet meetings.

3. the Cabinet is mostly concerned with ratifying decisions prepared in advance of the meeting.

4. sensitive items can be placed on the agenda.

5. the work of departments is coordinated at a high level.

D In order to be a member of the Cabinet, it is necessary to be
(1 answer)

1. appointed to a post in the Cabinet Secretariat.

2. invited by the Prime Minister to be the head of a major government department.

3. elected to a seat in the House of Commons.

4. appointed to a government office bearing the title of Secretary for State.

5. a member of either the House of Commons or the House of Lords, and appointed to a government office.

Answers to text comprehension tests

Test 1
(page 103)

Text extract 1

A = 2 and 4
B = 2 and 5
C = 4 and 5
D = 5

Text extract 2

A = 3
B = 3
C = 2 and 4
D = 2 and 5

Text extract 3

A = 1 and 4
B = 5
C = 2 and 4
D = 3 and 4

Test 2
(page 111)

Text extract 1

A = 2
B = 3
C = 4
D = 3

Text extract 2

A = 3
B = 3 and 4
C = 3
D = 5

Text extract 3

A = 3
B = 4
C = 1
D = 2 and 5

Test 3
(page 121)

Text extract 1

A = 2 and 3
B = 1
C = 2 and 4
D = 1 and 3

Text extract 2

A = 3 and 4
B = 3
C = 4 and 5
D = 2

Text extract 3

A = 5
B = 2
C = 2 and 3
D = 5

Visit Kogan Page on-line

Comprehensive information on
Kogan Page titles

Features include

- complete catalogue listings,
  including book reviews and
  descriptions

- on-line discounts on a variety
  of titles

- special monthly promotions

- information and discounts on
  NEW titles and BESTSELLING titles

- a secure shopping basket facility
  for on-line ordering

- infoZones, with links and
  information on specific areas of
  interest

PLUS everything you need to know
about KOGAN PAGE

http://www.kogan-page.co.uk